# The Bacchae

EURIPIDES

# The Frogs

ARISTOPHANES

# Crofts Classics

## GENERAL EDITOR

Samuel H. Beer, *Harvard University*

EURIPIDES

# The Bacchae

ARISTOPHANES

# The Frogs

*Two Plays of Dionysos*
*Translated and edited by*

## Francis Blessington

Northeastern University

Harlan Davidson, Inc.
Arlington Heights, Illinois 60004

1993

Library of Congress Cataloging-in-Publication Data

Euripides.
   [Bacchae. English]
   The Bacchae / Euripides. The frogs / Aristophanes; [both]
translated and edited by Francis Blessington.
     p.  cm. — (Crofts classics)
   "Two plays of Dionysos."
   Includes bibliographical references.
   ISBN 0-88295-129-7
   1. Greek drama—Translations into English. 2. Dionysus (Greek
deity)—Drama. I. Aristophanes. Frogs. 1993. II. Blessington,
Francis C., 1942– . III. Title.
PA3626.B58  1993
882'.01—dc20
                                    92-26669
                                       CIP

Manufactured in the United States of America

97 96 95 94 93 1 2 3 4 5                CM

For My Father
*In Memoriam*

# contents

# *preface*

I would like to thank Professor Bruce Donovan with whom I first studied *The Bacchae* and *The Frogs* in Greek at Brown University. More recently, Northeastern University earned my gratitude for a Student Service Project Grant, which helped produce a staged reading of *The Bacchae*. Particular thanks are owed to Marvin Lesser and Earl Harbert of the English Department for their support. Special credit must be given to Del Lewis, chair of the Department of Theatre and Dance, for taking time out of a heavy schedule to direct that production.

Thanks are due to both those who read parts in *The Bacchae* for me and those who read and commented upon the manuscript: Joseph Bashour, Joseph DeRoche, Harley and Richard Elia, Barbara Harrison, Julianna Mitchell, Leslie and Thomas Moore, Eric Ostrow, Raymond Papagno, Lisette Perelle, P. Carey Reid, Guy Rotella, Colette Sasso-Crandall, Theodore and Vas Vrettos, and Andrew Wolske.

Recently, I am indebted to The Greek Institute of Cambridge, Massachusetts, for sponsoring a public reading of my *Frogs*. I am particularly indebted to the director of the Institute, Athan Anagnostopoulos, for his interest in my work. I wish also to thank others who read the manuscript or took parts in this play: Maria and Demetra E. Anagnostopoulos, Michael Antonakes, Joseph DeRoche, Richard Elia, Nick Harris, Barbara Kapp, Willie Mahon, Meleti Pouliopoulos, P. Carey Reid, Guy Rotella, and Mary Anne Turiano.

Thanks also to those students who kept after me to teach them Greek both officially and unofficially. Their school, Northeastern University, provided me with a grant from The Research and Scholarship Development Fund, which helped me complete the translation of *The Frogs*.

Help with both plays also came from the reviewers and editors for the Crofts Classics Series and its publisher, Harlan Davidson, Inc.

As always, Ann Taylor has provided insightful commentary and immeasurable support, both as a wife and as a professor of English.

# introduction

## the bacchae: the coming of the god

> Will I set my bare foot
> Then in dancing vigils,
> Shake my throat in dewy air,
> Like a fawn in green joy
> Sporting in a meadow,
> When she's fled the fearful hunt . . .

In the Museum of Fine Arts in Boston there are two potsherds from a wine cooler dated 520 B.C.: one potsherd shows a female bacchant, a follower of the god Dionysos, rushing off, carrying a human leg; the other shows the mutilated body of King Pentheus, a legendary king who resisted the worship of Dionysos and who was torn apart by his own mother in a frenzy sent by the god. Pentheus had harassed the god's followers and was then himself subjected to the *sparagmos*, the rending of flesh, by the bacchants, though normally that of an animal. The two potsherds foreshadow two aspects of Dionysian worship: ecstasy and pain. Dionysos brings first the intoxication of being unselfconsciously and violently alive and then the agony of recognition and remorse.

This duality is also the pattern of all tragedy experienced by the Greek audience: fear of the ecstasy and pity for the agony. And tragedy stemmed from Dionysos' cult. But Euripides' play is not a rite, though it imitates one, nor an archetype or prototype of a mythical tragedy, but a play with contemporary themes. He makes the legend felt again, gives the characters a modern psychological reality,

and makes the myth of Dionysos new and eternal: the horror story with remorse, the full human experience of ecstasy and pain. For Euripides, the refusal of King Pentheus
to acknowledge the darker forces beneath the rational surface of life opens up the chaos below the surface of conscious reality, where life and death entwine, as in the lightning bolt that delivers Dionysos from Semele's womb and
kills her with the stroke. With Dionysos comes the madness
of his wine and of his dance.

Like all art, tragedy lessens the pain we feel: on the
potsherd, Pentheus smiles. The tragedy has its catharsis.
It also has its myth: an old legendary tale, far away in time,
its violence long over. As a work of art, the play symbol-
ically restricts and contains the force of the god. The art
is there to comfort us; the artistic control assures the reader
or viewer that all is only a tale. But this aesthetic barrier
is constantly under siege in the play. For the tale has its
immediacy in a way, and the characters who suffer are very
much like us. And though the punishing god is different
from us, something we can't control or understand, he is
as likely in us as outside of us. He stops and startles us,
like an empty mask. Even the aesthetic construction of the
play reflects the threat of Dionysian thought and action.

The story of a king who harassed Dionysos and his bacchants and who was punished was familiar to Homer three
centuries before Euripides (*Iliad* 6.130–140). Born in ap-
proximately 485 B.C., Euripides turned to this subject only
in the last two years of his life, when he was close to eighty
years old. He died in 406 B.C. after writing ninety-two
plays, of which nineteen are extant. Though written late,
*The Bacchae* shows no diminution of Euripides' power but
is a play central to Greek literature and thought. He composed it at the court of King Archelaus in Macedon in
northern Greece, where he may have witnessed more
primitive versions of Dionysos worship than were then al-
lowed at Athens in the state-tamed version of Dionysian
religion.

In the myth followed by Euripides, Dionysos was the
son of Zeus and a mortal, Semele, the daughter of Cadmus.
Cadmus had killed a dragon which had destroyed some of
his men. When Cadmus sowed the dragon's teeth in the

earth, the teeth grew into armed soldiers who killed each other, until five were left. Under Cadmus, they founded the city of Thebes.

The House of Cadmus, referred to in the play, is:

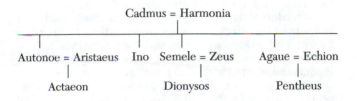

Cadmus = Harmonia

Autonoe = Aristaeus    Ino    Semele = Zeus    Agaue = Echion

Actaeon    Dionysos    Pentheus

Pentheus is a descendant of the dragon-born Echion and a cousin to Actaeon, who was torn apart by his own hunting dogs for boasting that he was a greater hunter than Artemis, an end that foreshadows Pentheus' own. Pentheus is also the cousin of Dionysos, and Dionysos is the grandson of Cadmus, whose ruling passion in the play is family pride.

The plot of *The Bacchae* (The Bacchants) is a "reintroduction" myth. Dionysos has established his rites in the East: in Lydia, near Mount Tmolus, and elsewhere in Asia Minor (modern Turkey). Now Dionysos, disguised as one of his own priests, returns with his Asian bacchants to Thebes, his birthplace, where he is not honored, but disclaimed as a god. Semele's family has refused to believe that she has had a child by Zeus. For punishment, Dionysos has driven the women of Thebes from their homes with madness. But he is resisted by King Pentheus.

At the beginning of the play, Pentheus is a typical tyrant of tragedy. So at first we sympathize with Dionysos and deplore the obtuseness of the king, who is incensed at Dionysos' worshippers, although they are rather harmless. Pentheus tries to capture the god and his followers. But then, later in the play, Dionysos' revenge makes us afraid of the god himself and of his dark power. We feel pity for Pentheus and his family because Dionysos drives them to such a pitch of "black maenadism."° As the true character of Pentheus is revealed, the force of Dionysos sweeps away

°A *maenad* is a *bacchant.*

all, including the philosophical discussions of the day about whether intellect can be superior to established custom. Nature alone rules. And Dionysos, terrifyingly enough, is part of nature. Moreover he is an eternal grain deity, who dies and returns from the dead, like his plants: the winter-blooming ivy and the fast-growing grape vine.

As readers of the play, we must keep in mind the striking and subversive effect of its stage presentation. The musical background is Dionysos' drum and flute. Dionysos' followers wear his fawnskin dress and carry his *thyrsos*, a long fennel reed, stuffed with vine leaves at the top, which they shake as they dance. The chorus, usually tangential to the action in a play by Euripides, is central to the effect and argument of this play because of its Dionysiac dancing. That these dancers are women is not surprising considering the servile status of women in ancient society. For them, Dionysos' liberating rites had a special appeal.

The play has lent itself to various historical interpretations. In Roman times, Plutarch recorded the gruesome chanting of lines from the play by an actor named Jason, who held up before his audience of Parthian soldiers the head of the Roman Crassus. The play was presented in America during Prohibition as a dramatization of the gangsterism that arose from the banning of alcohol. W. H. Auden and Chester Kallman did a libretto for Hans Werner Henze's operatic version of the play, *The Bassarids*. An African version was done by Wole Soyinka. At the time of this writing, a Japanese adaptation of the play is appearing at The New York Festival of the Arts.

But *The Bacchae* is not just drama; it is also a major contribution to Greek thought, for it warns of the emotion that Greek rationalism, prone to abstraction, was in danger of forgetting. Euripides reveals the deep feeling that Greek thinkers, liberating themselves from primitive superstition, tried to suppress. Intellectuals were insisting that one should live according to reason, propriety, even respectability. Reason, the charioteer, was expected to control the horses of emotion, later harnessing them with Plato's abstract Forms (*Phaedrus* 246–257; *Republic* 439–444) or with Aristotle's moderation (*Nicomachean Ethics* 1104). But reined-in spirits will break loose. If we think this too modern a view, we should remind ourselves what Freud learned from Greek literature. *The Bacchae* is a warning that Greek civilization should not place ideas before people. For Euripides, both politicians and intellectuals were ignoring the truths of experience, religion, custom, and nature. If they continued, something named Dionysos would be unleashed and tear apart society's fragile layer of rationality. Whatever this Dionysian force is, it extends beneath and beyond our conscious world. Envisioning this force, Euripides warned of the limits to classical thought.

# *the frogs*: the rebirth of Dionysos through comedy

> O Queen of holy rite,
> Demeter, stay and help
> To save your sacred chorus,
> And let me play in safety
> All day and dance.
>
> And grant me many jokes,
> Serious sayings too,
> To play, to mock, to conquer
> And wear the victor's garlands,
> Worthy your feast.

*The Frogs* of Aristophanes is the only extant Greek play other than *The Bacchae* of Euripides in which Dionysos is a major character. To read *The Frogs* and remember the Dionysos of *The Bacchae* is to feel the power of parody attempted by the tragedians in the satyr plays that they affixed to their tragic trilogies.° The god that is frightening in Euripides' play, worshipped in Athens, and central to the origin and sanctity of the Athenian theater is in Aristophanes a travesty of tragic heroism and a buffoon. In *The*

°Satyr plays were light dramas performed at the dramatic festivals.

*Frogs*, the effeminate god Dionysos, ludicrously disguised
as the hero Heracles, descends to the Underworld. Amidst
other absurd events, he spars in wit with his slave, Xanthias,
is whipped slapstick-style, and judges a clownish literary
contest between Aeschylus and Euripides. The myth of the
god is lowered to bathos: his disguise, his torture at the
hands of a mortal, his biennial death and resurrection, and
even the poetry of his ritual, are now treated with comic
degradation. We should remember that the play took place
in Dionysos' own theater in Athens, where his chief priest
sat in the front row of the audience and where the chorus
danced about Dionysos' own altar. Yet, in 405 B.C. at the
mid-winter Dionysian festival, the *Lenaea*, *The Frogs*, won
first prize and was later given a rare second performance.

Such license was characteristic of Old Comedy, of which
Aristophanes' plays are the sole survivors: eleven plays out
of perhaps forty-four. The plots are free-wheeling and un-
predictable fantasies. In his *Peace*, Trygaeus flies to Zeus'
house on the back of a dung beetle. Such constant surprise
so challenges the reader that students of Greek sometimes
despair of construing the translation of the next line, not
to mention the difficulties caused for the translator in re-
solving textual problems that have tormented editors for
millenia. Without the *scholia*, ancient commentaries on the
plays, it would be even more difficult to understand the
texts, although the extensive study of Aristophanes in an-
tiquity shows how appreciated his versatility and audacity
were. The many allusions in the plays constitute a similar
problem. They often necessitate footnotes for readers and
cuts or contemporizations for audiences. The translator,
however, must leave in these allusions.

The license of Aristophanic comedy led to its variety.
Aristophanes is a medley of parody, philosophy, politics,
poignancy, poetry, and nonsense. He is many-headed, and
translators must try to bring out his serious thought and
his lyricism as well as his more translatable buffoonery. To
Aristophanes, comedy can be a vehicle for the most important ideas. He wishes to teach and move as well as to
delight, so he creates a poetics of the unexpected: we do
not anticipate the sudden swerve from clowning to lyric
intensity or to philosophical insight. Moreover, these three

moods can be present at the same time, for the beautiful, the intellectual, and the funny are not always at odds in Aristophanes. Nor does he always dislike what he mocks. The Old Comedy, like Dionysos, presented opposites simultaneously. Several truths inhabit the gusto. In the opening scene of *The Frogs*, Aristophanes humorously indicts the verbal rigidities of the Sophists when Dionysos and his slave, Xanthias, discuss whether the donkey or Xanthias is carrying Xanthias' load since the donkey carries Xanthias.

But much of an older, religious rite remains. Aristophanes deepened the comedy of invective and slapstick abuse that preceded him and that derived from fertility ritual. The death of the old year, personified as the grain deity, was celebrated in the Athenian countryside where Aristophanes was born. The rites gave comedy its phalluses, its verbal license, its brawling characters, its emphasis upon eating, and its symbolic representation of rebirth. This play culminates in the ritual meal of communal unity. Even the early chorus of twelve may have represented the months. In any case, the comic world today remains the preserve of the unleashed and the unbuttoned.

The two most conspicuous peculiarities of Old Comedy may derive from these ritual roots. One is the *parabasis*, or "going aside," where the chorus doffs its masks and addresses the audience directly about political issues outside the framework of the play. Such addresses were urgent, for when *The Frogs* was performed, Athens was in its twenty-sixth year of the Peloponnesian War, a destructive struggle between Athens and Sparta, which Athens was to lose the following year. The war had begun when Aristophanes was about twenty and ended when he was about forty-five. His plays often reveal his constant striving for peace against Cleon and other members of the war party. He also uses the *parabasis* for his other causes, such as the emancipation of women and the preservation of traditional aspects of Athenian life. The *parabasis* alone could have recommended comedy to Aristophanes.

Another peculiarity is the centrality of the *agon* ("agony") or contest, which may derive from the ritual battle of the god with his adversaries. In *Lysistrata*, it is the battle of the sexes. In *The Frogs*, the *agon* is the contest between

Aeschylus and Euripides to establish poetic supremacy. Few but Aristophanes would risk, and succeed at, making great comedy out of literary criticism, out of the question of what makes great poetry. So his Euripides creates bombastic pastiches from Aeschylean tragedy, while his Aeschylus illustrates the low diction that he finds in Euripides' plays. The *agon* is thus elevated without losing the punch of the old ritual invective, libel, and assault.

After Aristophanes, comedy became domesticated to family drama. Its plots were no longer civic like those of Aristophanes. His ever-varied characters fossilized into the learned doctor, clever slave, braggart soldier, greedy old man, young rake, and courtesan of Middle and New Comedy, such as that of Menander, and have continued, after further taming, into modern film and television. But his tradition resurfaces in the comedy of such as Petronius, Lucian, Apuleius, Boccaccio, Chaucer, Rabelais, Cervantes, Shakespeare, Fielding, Sterne, and Joyce. Dionysos still returns, reborn in the vitality that makes great comedy.

# a note
# on the form
# of the plays

Greek drama is a highly stylized form of art. It is in meter and conforms to a pattern of alternating a dramatic *episodion* (scene made up of speeches) with a lyric *stasimon* (choral song or ode). In Greek, the speeches are usually in iambic trimeters, that is, three pairs of iambic feet (alternating a short and a long syllable, $- \cup$) or six iambs. Some variations are allowable, but the meter presents the sense of regularity, especially when contrasted with the great variety of meters found in the choral songs. These often consist of two stanzas of matching verse (*strophe* or "turn" and *antistrophe* or "counter-turn"). These two stanzas are followed by another stanza in a different meter (*epode* or "aftersong"). The chorus sang and danced the first two stanzas in parallel patterns and stood still for the *epode*. According to Nietzsche in *The Birth of Tragedy*, the alternation of dramatic verse and choral song represented the contrast between the Greek rationalism of Apollo and the emotionalism of Dionysos, an important contrast in *The Bacchae*.

Greek tragedy follows a predictable pattern, balancing violent emotions with clarity of form. Greek tragedy begins with a prologue followed by the *parodos*, or "entry-song" of the chorus. Then scenes alternate with choral songs, till the final *exodos* ("going-out") of the actors and chorus. The pattern in *The Bacchae*, along with corresponding line numbers, is:

| | |
|---|---|
| Prologue | (1–63) |
| Parodos | (64–169) |
| Scene I | (170–369) |
| Stasimon I | (370–433) |
| Scene II | (434–518) |
| Stasimon II | (519–575) |
| Scene III | (576–861) |
| Stasimon III | (862–911) |
| Scene IV | (912–976) |
| Stasimon IV | (977–1024) |
| Scene V | (1024–1152) |
| Stasimon V | (1153–1164) |
| Exodos | (1165–1392) |

Greek comedy follows a less predictable pattern than Greek tragedy, but is still very stylized. The prologue is followed by the *parodos* or "entry-song" of the chorus. Then scenes are interrupted by choral songs before and after the *parabasis* or "going aside." Then come more dramatic scenes with choral odes until the *exodos* or "going-out" of the actors and chorus. The pattern in *The Frogs*, with corresponding line numbers, is:

| | |
|---|---|
| Prologue | (1–322) |
| Parodos | (323–459) |
| Scenes with Choral Songs | (460–673) |
| Parabasis | (674–737) |
| Scenes with Choral Songs | (738–1499) |
| Agon | (begins 905) |
| Exodos | (1500–1533) |

Line numbers correspond to the Greek texts, but are not always consistent either in the Greek text or in the translation. Editors have deleted, added, and rearranged the lines of the Greek text, and I have occasionally expanded the number of lines in order to include as much as possible of the original text and sometimes contracted in order to gain poetic power. The original numbers are maintained for the sake of references to the text by scholars. Variations occur most often in the choral songs.

Greek choral song often employs responsion, parallel meters in corresponding stanzas. These Greek parallels and others I have mirrored in English meter, but I have not interrupted the text to indicate them. Changes in Greek meter are indicated by marginal shifts and by shifts in English meter.

# a note
# on the texts

For my translation of *The Bacchae*, I have used primarily Gilbert Murray's Oxford Classical Text, *Euripidis Fabulae*, Volume III (Oxford, Second Edition, 1913). At this time, Dr. James Diggle's new Oxford Classical Text is not yet available. I have also taken many textual readings from the commentary by E. R. Dodds, *Euripides: Bacchae* (Oxford, Second Edition, 1960).

In several places in the text of *The Bacchae*, there are possible lacunae. The largest and most certain gap is after line 1329, just before Dionysos begins his last prophecy ("You will be changed to a serpent"). Perhaps more than fifty lines spoken by Agaue and by Dionysos are missing. In the second dialogue between Dionysos and Pentheus, the line after line 651 is spurious ("An evil gift to make men delirious!"), but I have retained it for the necessary continuity. For a discussion of textual problems, see Dodds.

For my translation of *The Frogs*, I have followed primarily the Greek text of W. B. Stanford, *Aristophanes: The*

*[handwritten margin note:]* Dodds's Frogs

*[handwritten margin note:]* 50? lines missing

*[handwritten margin note:]* Stanford's Bacchae

*Frogs* (Macmillan, Second Edition, 1963). But I have dif-
fered from him on some points, including the attribution
of a couple of speeches. I have also used other editions,
especially V. Coulon's (Budé Series) and those others listed
in the Selected Bibliography.

# principal dates in the lives of

## Euripides

485? B.C.  Birth of Euripides at Phyla, a village near Athens.

480  Second Persian War: Athens sacked by Persians but defeats Xerxes at Salamis.

469  Birth of Socrates.

461–429  Golden Age of Athens under Pericles.

456  Death of Aeschylus.

455  First play, now lost, *The Peliades* ("Daughters of Pelias," part of the story of Medea) wins third prize in drama festival. Also early but undatable, *Rhesus* (Trojan War), if it is by Euripides.

447–432  Building of the Parthenon.

438  *Alcestis* (Heracles descends to Hades).

431  *Medea* (revenge play). Peloponnesian War begins: Athens vs. Sparta for the hegemony of Greece.

430?  *Heracleidae* ("Children of Heracles"). Plague in Athens.

429  Death of Pericles during plague.

428  *Hippolytus* (tragedy of cursed love).

426?  *Andromache* (Trojan War).

425?  *Hecuba* (Trojan War).

424?  *Suppliants* (Theban saga).

# Euripides and Aristophanes

## Aristophanes

450? B.C.   Birth of Aristophanes as an Athenian citizen
            during the Golden Age under Pericles.

429         Nicias is leader of aristocrats; Cleon leader of
            democrats.

427         *Daitales* ("Banqueters") produced (lost).
426         His *Babylonians* (lost) attacks magistrates, so Ar-
            istophanes is prosecuted by Cleon, a politi-
            cian of the war party.
425         *The Acharnians*, ("The Inhabitants of Achar-
            nae," a plea for peace).
424         *The Knights* attacks Cleon.

421?    *Cyclops* (only complete satyr [parodic] play; cf. Homer's *Odyssey*, IX.)

417?    *Heracles*.
415     *The Trojan Women*.

413?    *Electra* (aftermath of Trojan War).

412?    *Iphigenia in Tauris* (aftermath of Trojan War). *Helen* (of Troy). *Ion* (romance of discovery of lost child).
411     Revolution of Four Hundred. Democracy abolished, but restored next year.

410?    *Phoenissae* ("Phoenician Women," Oedipus legend).
408     *Orestes* (aftermath of Trojan War). Goes to the Court of Argelaus at Pella in Macedonia, in northern Greece.
406     Dies at Pella. Death of Sophocles.
405?    Posthumous performance of *Iphigenia at Aulis* (Trojan War) and *The Bacchae*.

423      *The Clouds* ridicules Socrates as teacher of false rhetoric.

422      *The Wasps* satirizes the jury system.

421      *Peace* (with Sparta). Peace of Nicias, a treaty with Sparta.

420      Alcibiades rises to power.

418      War renewed with Sparta.

414      *The Birds* (a fantasy of escape).

413      Sicilian Expedition ends in disaster. Alcibiades goes over to Spartan side.

411      *Lysistrata* ("Demobilizer" calls a sex strike, which ends the war). *Thesmophoriazusae* ("Women at the Thesmophoria Festival" gather to punish Euripides).

405      *The Frogs* (Dionysos descends to Hades; debate between Aeschylus and Euripides).      Frogs 405 BC

404      Fall of Athens to Sparta.

399      Execution of Socrates.

392      *Ecclesiazusae* (The "Women in the Assembly" take over Athens).

388      *Plutus* ("The God of Wealth," Comedy of Manners: New Comedy begins).      New Comedy

385?      Death of Aristophanes.

# The Bacchae

# Euripides

# Characters

_Dionysus_

DIONYSOS, *also called Bromios and Bacchos*
CHORUS OF BACCHANTS, *The Bacchae, Asian women, followers of Dionysos. Also called Maenads* Χορὸς Βακχῶν
TEIRESIAS, *a blind prophet*
CADMUS, *founder of Thebes*
PENTHEUS, *King of Thebes, grandson of Cadmus*
SOLDIER, *one of Pentheus' guards* Θεράπων
FIRST MESSENGER, *a herdsman* Ἄγγελος
SECOND MESSENGER, *a servant of Pentheus* ὕστερος Ἄγγελος

_Agave_

AGAUE, *mother of Pentheus*
SERVANTS OF CADMUS *(silent parts)*

*(Scene: In front of the royal palace at Thebes in central Greece. On stage is a tomb from which smoke rises. Dionysos enters.)* Ἥκω Διὸς παῖς τήνδε Θηβαίων χθόνα

DIONYSOS. I, Dionysos, have come to Thebes,
Zeus' son, whom Cadmus' daughter,
Semele, bore and delivered by lightning.
Changed from a god to a man,
I visit the streams of Dirce and Ismenos,                    5
And see the grave of my thunder-bolted mother
And her ruined home still smoking
With Zeus' live flame—Hera's
Deathless hate against Semele.
I honor Cadmus who made this spot                            10
Sacred to his daughter's tomb,
And I have covered it with fresh vine.

I have left behind the golden lands of Lydia
And Phrygia, crossed the sun-beaten highlands
Of Persia and Bactria's walled cities,                       15
Gray Media, lush Arabia—
By the salt sea all through Asia,
Which marries Greek and barbarian to one race
In thriving, high-towered cities,
And I have come to this Greek city,                          20
After having set Asia dancing
To my rites, to show my godhead.

I have cried Thebes awake first
In Greece, fastened my fawnskin to the flesh,
Handed on the ͺthyrsos,ͺ my ivy spear.                        25

**3, Semele.** Pregnant with Dionysos, she was killed by a lightning bolt from her lover, Zeus, but their child was preserved. Cf. "introduction."
**5, Dirce and Ismenos.** Theban rivers.
**13–17.** Dionysos tells of his journey east from the Aegean. Lydia and Phrygia are in Asia Minor (Turkey). Persia and Media are in modern Iran. Bactria was further east.
**24–25, fawnskin . . . thyrsos.** For the wearing of the fawnskin and the ritual wand, the *thyrsos*, see "introduction."

3

4   *Euripides*

Revenge
for slander
by Semele's
sisters

Their
madness

women of
Thebes

When my mother's sisters foolishly
Denied Dionysos to be Zeus-born,
They rumored Semele mated with a mortal
And blamed Zeus for the guilty bedding—
30  Cadmus' scheme, they said—and boasted
Zeus killed her for her lies.
So I have whipped them to madness.
Possessed and homeless, they dwell in the mountains,
Forced to wear my animal livery.
35  The whole female seed of Cadmus,
Every woman, I have driven outdoors
To rage, mingled with Cadmus' own daughters
Among green fir and open rocks.
For this city must know, in spite of itself,
40  That it is ignorant of Bacchic rites
And that I must defend Semele, I
Whom she bore to Zeus, a revelation to mankind.

Pentheus
is king

Now Cadmus has crowned Pentheus king,
The son born to his daughter, who wars
45  Against me, a god banished
From his worship and missing in his prayers.
For this I'll reveal my divine nature
To all. Once I right this city,
I'll set foot in another land
50  And make myself known. But if Thebes tries
To battle my bacchants off the mountain,
I'll assemble a maenad army against them.
So I have assumed mortal shape
And transformed a god into a man.

Tmolus,
Lydia,
Phrygia

55  But, O my bacchants, once of Tmolus,
The barricade of Lydia, sisters whom I led
From the barbarians, my friends and comrades,
Raise up your Phrygian tambourines,

**55, Tmolus.** A mountain range in Lydia.

My gift and the Great Mother's, Cybele.
Circle King Pentheus' house!
Ring out so Thebes may hear!                                    60

*back to Cithaeron*

Now I go to Cithaeron's glens
To join the chorus with my bacchants.
*(Exit.* CHORUS *enters.)*
  CHORUS.      From Asian land, I left Ἀσίας ἀπὸ γαίας   PARODOS
      The sacred mountain and spur on     65 *modified ionic a min.*
      The sweet pain of the Roaring God,    *Str. 1*
  His toiless toil, and cry his Dionysian "Evoe!"

     Who, who stands in the road?    *Ant. 1*
    Let him be deep indoors and each
      Man purify a holy tongue,    70
For I shall hymn Bacchos in the eternal way.

                            *Str. 2*
       His fortune's blest
      Who knows God's rites;
      Serves with his life;
      And twins his soul    75
      With mountain revels,
        Purifications,
      And lawful ritual
      Of the Great Mother;
      Flashing his thyrsos,    80
       An ivy-crowned
      Bacchic servant.

    Dance, Bacchants, dance.
    Bring home the Roarer,
      God-child of God.    85
    From Phrygian mountains

**59, Cybele.** A near-Eastern goddess, whose worship became associated with Dionysos. Also called Rhea and the Great Mother (below).
**62, Cithaeron.** A mountain range south of Thebes.
**67, "Evoe."** The traditional Bacchic cry.

To wide Greek streets,
Bring Dionysos.


*Ant. 2*
*birth of D.*

He whom his mother,
Stricken with labor
90        Drove from her womb
With Zeus' thunder
And yielded life
To the bright wound.
Zeus took him quickly
95        Into the womb
Of his thigh, covered,
Sealed with gold pins,
Hidden from Hera.


Then Zeus bore him,
100        The Fates perfected
*bull,* A bull-horned god,
*snake* Crowned with a snake-crown:
So maenads braid
Their wild trophies.


*Str. 3*  105        O Thebes, nurse of Semele,
With ivy hood yourselves,
Abound, abound with bryony,
The evergreen and fruitful,
And consecrate yourselves with sprigs
110        Of oak and silver fir;
Fringe the spotted fawnskin dress
With locks of wooly hair;
Be wise in wielding the wild thyrsos.
Now all the land shall dance—
115        The leader will play the Roaring God.
εἰς ὄρος εἰς ὄρος Mountains, to the mountains!

**107, bryony.** A climbing plant derived from the Greek work for
"to abound with."

There many, far from beam and shuttle,
Wait, crazed by Dionysos.


O cave of the Curetes,                                    120 Ant. 3
The sacred Cretan precinct,
The chambers that gave birth to Zeus,
In there they found my drum,                              Corybantes
The triple-crested Corybantes,                            & drum
The circlet of stretched leather,                         125
Sweetened the drum with Phrygian fluting
Into the maenad whirl,
And set in Mother Rhea's hand
To beat out Bacchic shouts.
Then frenzied satyrs gained the drum                      130
Borrowed from the Mother,
And joined the Feast of Double Years,
The Chorus Bacchos loves.


Welcome he is in the mountains,                           135 Epode
Falling from the swift bands
Earthward, wrapped in holy fawnskin,
Seizing the slaughtered goat's blood,
Joyous eating of flesh still raw,
Storming Lydian mountains,                                140
Leader Dionysos, "Evoe!"
Earth reeks nectar, wine, milk.                           nectar, wine,
Dionysos' celebrant swings                                milk
High the pine torch smoking,                              pine
Like the incense of Syria,                                145
Streaming from its holder,

**120, the Cretan Curetes or Corybantes.** Priests of Cybele (see note
on line 59) who were supposed to have invented the kettledrum
to keep the cries of the infant Zeus from being heard by his father,
Kronos, who wished to devour him. The flute and the drum are
the musical instruments of Dionysian worship. Cf. "introduction."
**132, Feast of Double Years.** Dionysos was worshipped in a mid-
winter biennial festival.

As he rushes and he dances,
Goading on the sluggards,
Urging them faster with his cries.
150  Wind tossing his soft locks, he
Roars over the Bacchic shouting:


"Dance, dance, Bacchants!
In the glint of gold-streamed Tmolus,
155  Hymn the god with drumbeats,
Glory Bacchus with his evoes,
Phrygian cries and calling,
160  When the sweet and holy pipe roars
Solemn sport, that joins your
165  Mountain-roaming in the mountains."
Gleeful as a filly
In a pasture with her mother,
Hurling her swift legs, the bacchant leaps.

*(Enter* TEIRESIAS, *blind.)*

EPISODE 170  TEIRESIAS.  Who's at the gate? Call Cadmus out,
Teiresias  The son of Agenor, who abandoned Sidon
& Cadmus  To raise these towers of the Theban citadel.
Someone go, announce Teiresias
Wants him. He knows well why
175  I've come, and what I, an old man,
Have devised for him, even older:
thyrsus  To tie the thyrsos and knot the fawnskin,
& ivy  And crown his head with ivy growth.

*(Enter* CADMUS.*)*

CADMUS.  O friend, I hear and know your voice,
The wise sound of a wise man.
180  I come, ready in the dress of the god.
Because he is my daughter's child,
Dionysos, who showed men he is god,
We must increase his power all we can.
185  Where must we dance? Where set our feet

**172, Agenor . . . Sidon.** Cadmus' father had left Sidon in Phoenicia, at the eastern end of the Mediterranean.

And shake gray hairs? Advise, Teiresias,
An old man to an old man, for you are wise,
So, neither day nor night,
Shall I weary of striking the ground with my thyrsos.
That I am old, I sweetly forgot.

   TEIRESIAS.  You feel the same as I then:
Returned to prime and yearning for the chorus.     190

   CADMUS.  Shall we call a carriage for the mountain?

   TEIRESIAS.  The god is not honored that way.

   CADMUS.  One graybeard shall toddle another.

   TEIRESIAS.  The god shall speed us there with ease.

   CADMUS.  Will we alone dance for Bacchos?     195

   TEIRESIAS.  Only we think right. The others vilely.

   CADMUS.  Delay is tedious. Take my hand.

   TEIRESIAS.  There! Take it and yoke them together.

   CADMUS.  Being mortal, I do not slight the gods.*

   TEIRESIAS.  We do not outwit the gods either.     200

From our fathers we received timeless truths
That no cleverness can overthrow,
Whatever wisdom wise men uncover.
Who won't say I disgrace old age
Going to dance, crowned with ivy?     205
But no, the god does not keep
Young or old from his forced dance,
But wishes honor from all alike,
And to grow great, excluding no one.

   CADMUS.  Since you, Teiresias, can't see the light,     210
I shall be your seer in words.

Pentheus is coming home posthaste,
Echion's son, whom I made king.
How he hurries! What news does he have?
*(Enter* PENTHEUS.)

   PENTHEUS.  Even abroad, out of the country, I heard     215
Of the strange corruption in the city:
Our women have abandoned our homes
And, in a jacked-up frenzy of phony inspiration,

*οὐ καταφρονῶ 'γὼ τῶν θεῶν θνητὸς γεγώς

off to
Cithaeron

only two
men
who
honor D.

no shame

none
excluded

Pentheus

Riot in the dark mountains,
Honoring this upstart god, Dionysos—

*τὸν νεωστὶ δαίμονα*
*Διόνυσον, ὅστις ἔστι·*

*wine &*
*lust* 220   Whatever he is—dancing in his chorus.
Full jugs of wine stand in their midst
And each woman slinks off
To the wilderness to serve male lust,
Pretending they are raving priestesses,
225   But Aphrodite leads them, not Bacchos.

*some women*
*captured*   So, as many as I have taken,
My men hold bound in the common jail.
Those who are free I'll hunt from the mountains,
*Agave, Ino,*
*Autonoe are*   Ino, and Agaue, who bore me to Echion,
*freed* 230   And Actaeon's mother, I mean Autonoe.
Binding them in iron nets,
I'll soon end these promiscuous rites.

*Pentheus'*
*view*   They say some stranger has come,
A fraudulent sorcerer from Lydia
235   Who combs his good curls with perfume
And has Aphrodite's charms in his wine-flushed eyes.
Holding out his joyful mysteries,
He mingles with young women day and night.
If I get him within this house,
240   I'll halt his drumming thyrsos and shaking
*he'll*
*decapitate*
*him*   Hair, by lopping head from body.

*He* says Dionysos is a god,
That he was sewn in Zeus' thigh,
The one consumed by lightning-fire with his mother
245   Who lied about sex with Zeus.
Are these things not worthy of the gibbet,
Outrageous outrages, whoever the stranger is?

Now I spy another wonder,

**229–30, Echion, Actaeon, Autonoe.** For Pentheus' family, see "introduction."

Teiresias, the visionary in dappled fawnskins,
And my mother's father, my laughingstock,                    250
Revelling with a fennel reed.

               Sir,
I abhor looking at your witless old age.
Will you not throw off this ivy? Not free
Your hand of the thyrsos, grandfather?

You persuaded him, Teiresias, you hope*                      255
By bringing in another new god
To augur and charge for fire-divination.
If old age did not save you,
You would squat chained in the middle of the bacchants
For importing these wicked rites.                            260
I say that feast where a woman takes
The gleaming grape is most diseased. τῆς δυσσεβείας, ὦ ξένε
    CHORUS. What impiety! O stranger, do you not respect
The gods and Cadmus who sowed the soldier-race?
Does Echion's child shame his people?                        265
    TEIRESIAS. When some wise man has a fair cause
To present, to speak well is easy. οὐ μέγ' ἔργον εὖ λέγειν
You have a tongue, glib *like* thought,
But no sense lies in your words.
The man that rashness prompts to speak                       270
Proves an evil citizen and senseless.

This new divinity that you mock—
My words are too weak to proclaim how great
He shall grow in Greece. Two things, young man,
Are first among mankind: Demeter,                            275
She's the Earth—call her by either name—
Who nourishes mortals with dry food.
The other, who came after, the seed
Of Semele, discovered Demeter's wet rival,
The drink of the grape, brought it to man                    280
To ease pain for suffering mortals,
When they are filled with the flowing vine,
And to give sleep, forgetful of daily ills.

*cf. Oedipus & Creon

[margin annotations:] Peutheus rebukes Teiresias | observe piety & hospitality | glib but not wise | two greatest: Dion. & Demeter (Earth)

There is no other cure for pain.
This god is poured out to gods!
285 So men owe him all their good.

*Teir.*
*rationalizes*
*thigh myth*

Do you now mock him sewn
In Zeus' thigh? I'll explain that truth:   μηρός
When Zeus snatched him from the lightning-flame
And brought the baby, a god, to heaven,
290 Hera wished to fling him from the sky,
But Zeus plotted back, as a god can.
He broke off a part of the surrounding ether,
And made a phantom Dionysos for Hera,
A sky-piece for her anger. In time,   μέρος
295 Men said he was Zeus' "thigh-piece,"
Confounding the term, because the god
Was Hera's "sky-piece," and constructed a tale.   ὅμηρος & μηρ?

*god of*
*prophecy*

This divinity is a prophet, for frenzied
Rites and mania have mantic greatness.
300 As the god enters full the body,
He makes the mad speak the future.
He also shares a part of Ares' realm,
When fear without a blow strikes
To panic an army deployed and armed.
305 This madness too derived from Bacchos.
You'll see him yet on Delphi's rocks,
Leaping the twin-peaked tableland with torches,
Swinging and brandishing the Bacchic branch
—so great in Greece!

But hear me, Pentheus.
310 Don't presume that power rules mankind,
Nor, if you think sick thoughts,
That you think well. Receive the god here,

**297, sky-piece.** The Greek pun is a confusion between *ho mēros*
(thigh) and *homeros* (hostage, i.e., the dummy made of ether was
a hostage of Hera's).
**299, mantic.** Having the power of a prophet. The word is histor-
ically related to *maenad*, *mania*, and *maniac*.

Pour offerings, revel, crown your head.

Dionysos does not compel women
To be chaste in love, but chastity dwells
Always and everywhere in human nature.
You must look for it there. Even in the rites,
The pure will not corrupt herself.

315 *woman's chastity*

You notice and rejoice when many linger
At your gates, and the city hails "Pentheus!"
He too, I believe, loves to be honored.
So I and Cadmus, whom you mock,
Will crown ourselves with ivy and dance,
A grizzled couple, but dance we must.
⌊Your words can't make me fight gods.⌋
Such rage is most cruel and incurable.
No drug can help you, already drugged.

*Dion. wants honor too*

320

*Teiria Cad. will dance*

325

CHORUS. Old man, your words don't shame the god.
Lowly wise, you honor great Bromios.

CADMUS. My son, Teiresias advised you well.
Be home with us, not outside the laws.
Now you fly off. Your thought is thoughtless.
If he is no god, as you claim,
Let it be said he is, and wisely lie
That he exists and Semele is his mother.
Then family honor will be all ours.*

330

*even if D. isn't divine, the honor*
335 *is worth it all*

You know ⌊Actaeon's painful fate,⌋
Torn to rags by the flesh-eating dogs
He raised, for boasting in the mountain precincts
He was mightier in the hunt than Artemis.
Don't suffer like him! Here, I'll crown you
With ivy. Give honor with us to the god.

*head exemplum of Actaeon*

340

PENTHEUS. Will you unhand me and go revel?
Not stain me with your foolishness?
I'll bring that professor of folly to justice.

345

**340, Artemis.** Goddess of the hunt.

*not Cadmus' admission that he doubts D.'s divinity, but merely a trick to get P. to stay out of trouble*

Let someone go as quickly as he can
And pry up the seat of this seer's auguries
With crowbars, topple and upend it,
Confound all helter-skelter,   *ἄνω κάτω*
350   Throw sacred fillets to rain and wind.
Doing this I'll bite deepest.

Others track through the state
The dainty stranger who infects our women   *θηλύμορφον ξένον*
With a new disease and pollutes our beds.
355   Take him, and bring him bound
*death*   Before me, so he may die justly
*warrant*   Through stoning—a bitter carouse in Thebes!
        TEIRESIAS.  Poor man, you don't know where your
            words lead.
    Before, you were mindless. Now you are insane.

360   Let us go, Cadmus, and plead
For him, though he be savage,
And for the city, that the god do nothing
Strange. Come with your ivy stick,
Try to restore my strength and I'll yours.
365   Two old men falling is disgusting.
But so? We must be slaves to Bacchos.
*pun*   Let Pentheus, whose name means sorrow, not bring *that*   *πένθος*
To your house, Cadmus. I speak no prophecy,
Just fact. For a fool speaks folly.
    *(They go out.)*

STASIMON 370   CHORUS.   O *Holiness*, Queen of the Gods,   *Ὀσία πότνα θεῶν*
1                O *Holiness*, across the land
str. 1               You pass your golden wing.
            Did you perceive the words of Pentheus?
            Did you not hear unholy hybris
375         Against the Roaring God, Semele's son,
            First god of all the blest, and crowned

**350, sacred fillets.** Woolen ribbons hung up to consecrate a seat
of divination. (Dodds)
**374, hybris.** Insolence or outrage.

With joy and beauty, he whose way
Is merging with the dance
And smiling to the flute                        380
To set an end to pain,
When gods feast and the gleaming grape
Arrives or the wine bowl throws sleep
On ivy-wreathed and revelling men?              385

For those who wield unbridled tongues,          Ant. 1
For those who love a heedless mind,
Misfortune is the end.
The life of calmness, the unshaken thought,     390
Remains, and keeps a house unruined.
Though far away the Titans dwell in heaven,
Nevertheless they note men's deeds.
But shallow wisdom is untrue.                   395  *human*
To think beyond this life                             *brevity &*
Cuts short our life. He who                           *limit*
Pursues the great, forfeits
What lies at hand. Such temperaments,
According to my thought, belong                 400
To madmen and the ill-advised.

Let me fly to Cyprus,                           Str. 2  X
Island of Aphrodite,                            *Cyprus*
Where the love gods dwell,                      405
Charming mortal hearts,
And to Paphos where the hundred-mouthed,
Rainless streams of a barbarian river
Fertilize the fields.
And Pieria, seat of the muses,                  410
Gift of beauty, holy

**393, the Titans.** Sons of Uranus, who here represent the gods in general.

**407, Paphos.** The center of the worship of Aphrodite on the island of Cyprus.

**410, Pieria.** An area of Macedonia in northern Greece associated with the Muses, goddesses of the arts.

Slope of Olympus.
Bromios, Bromios, take me there—
Bacchant, leader, demon—
There the Graces revel,
415         There Desire carouses, and
Custom makes us right.

*Ant. 2*

God, the child of Zeus,
Joying in festival,
*P. loves peace*
Loves *Peace*, giver of treasure,
420         Child-nurturing goddess.
Dionysos gives poor and rich alike
Equal pleasure in the winecup, assuaging
Every grief, and hates
Those unmindful of *these* precepts:
425         Day and blessed night,
Live in gladness,
And withhold the mind and wise heart
From the prideful mockers.
430         What the crowd of commoner
Folk conjecture and approve—
That I would accept.

(SOLDIER *enters stage left with* DIONYSOS. PENTHEUS *enters right.*)

*EPISODE 2*
SOLDIER. Pentheus, we have hunted down the quarry
435    You wanted, nor did we race in vain.
We took him calm, nor did he pull back
His foot in flight, but willing gave his hands,
Nor turned pale, nor altered his ruddy cheek.
Smiling, he let us bind him, waited
*stranger did not resist* 440    To be led away and made work easy.
From shame I spoke, "O Stranger, unwilling
I take you, by Pentheus' order who sent me."

But the jailed bacchants, the ones you snared
*women have been freed*    And clapped in chains in the public dungeon,
445    Are loose and fled to the mountain glades,
Leaping and calling Bromios, their god.

~ *stranger* ~

By themselves the chains dropped from their feet
And door-bars fell by no mortal hand.
This man of many miracles has come here
To Thebes. But the rest is your care.                              450
*(Exit.)*

    PENTHEUS.  Set free his hands. Being in my net,
He shall not be so quick to flee.


Stranger, your figure is not unpleasing—                    P. appraises
To women, your purpose in coming to Thebes.                  stranger
Such flowing tresses are not for wrestling,                        455
Pouring over this cheek, full of desire.
You have a fair face from your art,
Not from the sun's rays, from the shadows
Where you stalk Aphrodite with your beauty.


First, tell me, what is your race?                                 460
    DIONYSOS.  I'll not hold back. It is easily told.
You have heard of flowery Tmolus.                           stichomythia
    PENTHEUS.  I know the mountains that circle Sardis.    463–508
    DIONYSOS.  I am from there. Lydia is my home.
    PENTHEUS.  Why have you brought your rites to
      Greece?                                                 465
    DIONYSOS.  Dionysos sent us, the Child of Zeus.       same Zeus
    PENTHEUS.  What Zeus *there* begets new gods?
    DIONYSOS.  The same that married Semele here.
    PENTHEUS.  Did he compel you in dreams or daylight?
    DIONYSOS.  Face to face, he presented his mysteries.   470
    PENTHEUS.  Your mysteries, what form do they take?
    DIONYSOS.  For the profane to know is unthinkable!
    PENTHEUS.  What pleasure do they bring his
      worshippers?
    DIONYSOS.  Not lawful for you to know, but worth
      knowing.
    PENTHEUS.  You counterfeit well, so I'll want to hear.  475

**462, Tmolus.** See note on line 55.
**463, Sardis.** The capital of Lydia.

DIONYSOS.   The god's rites loathe the impious.

PENTHEUS.   What was this god you say you saw clearly?

DIONYSOS.   Whatever he chose. I did not limit him.

PENTHEUS.   Another diversion. Clever and meaningless.

480    DIONYSOS.   To the ignorant, wisdom will seem folly.

PENTHEUS.   Did you bring the god here first?

DIONYSOS.   All foreigners dance his rites.

*matter of customs, not knowledge*    PENTHEUS.   They understand far less than Greeks.

DIONYSOS.   Rather more in this, though custom differs. *νομοι*

485    PENTHEUS.   Do you worship in daylight or at night?

DIONYSOS.   Mostly at night. Darkness is most sacred.

PENTHEUS.   That is treacherous and unwholesome for women.

*sharp exchange*    DIONYSOS.   Some find shame even in daylight.

PENTHEUS.   You, you must pay for these base sophistries!

490    DIONYSOS.   And you for stupidity and sacrilege against the god!

PENTHEUS.   How insolent the priest, and skilled in words.

DIONYSOS.   Tell what horror I must suffer.

*he'll cut his hair*    PENTHEUS.   First I'll cut your love-locks.

DIONYSOS.   My curls are sacred. I nourish them for the god.

*thyrsos* 495    PENTHEUS.   Then, hand over that thyrsos.

DIONYSOS.   Take it yourself. It belongs to Dionysos.

PENTHEUS.   In a prison, we shall guard your person.

DIONYSOS.   The god releases me when I wish.

PENTHEUS.   When you call from *among* the Bacchants.

500    DIONYSOS.   Nearby even now, he is watching my suffering.

PENTHEUS.   Where? Not present to my eye.

DIONYSOS.   With me. Being ungodly you can't see.

PENTHEUS.   Seize him. He scorns me and the city.

DIONYSOS.   Sane, I forbid you madmen to bind me.

505    PENTHEUS.   But I shall, having more power than you.

DIONYSOS.   You are ignorant of life, of what you do, and what you are. οὐκ οἶσθ' ὅ τι ζῆις, οὐδ' ὃ δρᾷς, οὐδ' ὅστις εἶ.

PENTHEUS.  I'm Pentheus, Child of Agaue and Echion.
DIONYSOS.  You are worthy of your luckless name:
   Sorrow.
PENTHEUS.  Go! Lock him in the stables close by,
So he may meditate the mysterious dark.* 510
Dance there! The women you brought,
Your companions in sin, I shall sell off,
*(sound of drums from* CHORUS*)*
Or, taking those hands from the thumping drum,
I shall make slaves for my loom.
   DIONYSOS.  I come. For what is not to be I'll not 515
Suffer. But, Dionysos, whom you say is not,
Pursues you, a punishment for your outrages.
For violating us, you imprison him.
*(They go out.)*
   CHORUS.       Achelous' Daughter, Ἀχελώου θύγατερ     STASIMON
        Royal Dirce, Blessed Maiden, ˘ ˘ – ˘ ˘ – ˄   2
               *Ion. a minore*   520 str.
           You once in your streams      D.'s birth
             Took the child of Zeus
When he snatched him from the deathless lightning,
      Hid him in his thigh to bear him,
         Wailing loud these words: 525
         "Go, my dithyramb, into
       My male womb. O Bacchos,
With this name I reveal you to Thebes."


         But You, Holy Dirce, 530
        Shove me away who hold
      On your banks the wreathed bands.
      Why do you forsake me? Why flee?
         Yet still, for Bacchos'
          Favoring vine, you shall 535
         Care for Bromios still.


**519–20 Achelous.** The name of an important river god and of the
largest river in Greece. **Dirce.** See note on line 5.
**526, dithyramb.** A term for Dionysos and for his dance.
**532, wreathed.** The bacchants wore ivy crowns.

*D. will be shut up, as he was in Zeus's thigh.

Ant.

P.'s birth

Earth-born child, the dragon's  ‒ ‒ ‒ ⊢ ‒ ‒
Seed, Pentheus shows his root,
540 Whom the snakeman, Echion,
Begot, hideous monster,
Not of human race, and like a blood-spattered
Giant, adversary to gods.
545 Quickly he shall bind me,
Bromios' servant, snared.
Now he hides my fellow-
Reveller inside a darkened room.

550 Do you see this, Child of
Zeus, O Dionysos,
Your preachers, in the agonies
Of torture? O come, Lord, shaking
High your gold-faced thyrsos
Down Olympus, bridle
555 This man's murderous pride.

Epode

Where then, on Nysa, nurse  ∪∪ ‒ ‒ |∪∪ ‒ ‒
Of beasts, O Dionysos,
Or on Corycian heights,
Do you bear high your thyrsos
Over your revelling bands?

560 Perhaps, upon Olympus,
Within its dense-leafed chambers,
Where Orpheus once harped,
And with his song he drove

**537–40, Earth-born . . . Echion.** For Echion and his descent from
a dragon, see Introduction. In Greek, *drakōn* means both "dragon"
and "snake." *Echion* means "Snake man."
**556–57, Nysa . . . Corycian.** Nysa is the name of several sights
sacred to Dionysos and may derive from the last part of the god's
name. The cave of Corycia was on Mount Parnassus near Delphi.
**560, Olympus.** Mountain home of gods and goddesses in northern
Greece.
**562, Orpheus.** God of music and poetry.

Together beasts and trees.

O fortunate Pieria,   ᵛᵇ↩ᵛᵛᵛ‒     565
God honors you,
Will come to set you dancing
In Bacchic revelry,
Will goad his whirling maenads     570
Across fast-flowing Axius,

Across the Ludias,
Father of happiness,
Giver of wealth to men.
I've heard he gilds his land
With loveliest water, joy of horses.     575
                      EPISODE 3

DIONYSOS (*offstage*).    Io!   ἰώ
      Hear my voice! Hear!   ᵛᵛᵛ‒|ᵛᵛᵛ‒
ἰὼ Βάκχαι   Io, Bacchants. Bacchants! Io!
CHORUS. (1) Who is this? Who? Where does
      Dionysos' voice call me from?
DIONYSOS.    Io! Io! Once again I call,     580
      Child of Zeus, Semele's son.
CHORUS. (2)    Io! Master! Master!
      Come now into our band.
      Bromios, O Bromios!
DIONYSOS. Goddess Earthquake, shake the floor of    earthquake
   earth!                               585
INDIVIDUAL CHORAL VOICES. (3)
        —Ha! Aha! ἂ ἂ
      Swiftly Pentheus' house will
      Shake apart in ruins.

(4)     —Dionysos is inside the palace.
    Honor him!
(5)        —O, how we honor him!     590

(6)    —See how, there, those marble lintels

**565, Pieria.** See note on line 410.
**571–72, Axius and the Ludias.** Macedonian rivers.

On the columns break apart?
Bromios shouts within the building!

*lightning* 595   DIONYSOS. Fire the gleaming thunder torch.*

Burn, burn Pentheus' palace.

CHORUS. (6)               Ah! Ah!

Do you not see fire, distinguish
Not about Semele's tomb the lightning
That she left, flame of thunder-throwing Zeus?

600               Hurl your trembling bodies
To the ground! Hurl them, Maenads.
For our lord assails this palace,
Setting it on end, our child of Zeus.

*(Enter DIONYSOS.)*

*troch.*
*tetram.*
*catal.* 605   DIONYSOS. Women of Asia, thus full of fear $-\upsilon-\upsilon|-\upsilon-|-\upsilon-\upsilon|-\upsilon-\wedge$
And fallen to the ground? It seems you felt
Bacchos destroy the palace, but arise!
Come, put the trembling away from your limbs.

*(Coryphaeus?)*   CHORUS. O great light of our revels,
How happily I see you. I was alone.

610   DIONYSOS. Did you despair when I was sent
To ruin in Pentheus' dark traps?
CHORUS. What else? Who was my guard, if you met
     misfortune?
But how did you escape the sinner?
DIONYSOS. I saved *myself*, easily, without pain.
CHORUS. Did he not bind your hands in strong
615     knots?
DIONYSOS. So I mocked him: seeming to bind me,
He neither held nor touched me, but fed

*epiphanies*
*plagues*
*Pentheus*   On hope. Spotting a ⌊bull⌋ in the stall
Where he would pen me, he shackled its knees
620   And hooves, puffing rage, dropping sweat,
Chewing his lip. I sat calm,
And watched. Meanwhile Bacchos came
And shook down the palace and kindled
His mother's tomb. When Pentheus looked,
He thought he saw the ⌊house afire,⌋ darted about
625   Ordering slaves to bring a river of water.

*glory that killed Semele

All were wedded to the work—for nothing!
Shirking this job, since he thought I fled,
He flew in, snatching a black sword,
But Bromios, it seemed (it's my opinion),
Created a phantom in the courtyard; at this       630
He rushed and stabbed the luminous air,
As if slaughtering me. Bacchos added
Outrage to outrage; he shattered down
The house. All is ruin, as Pentheus
Looks most bitterly on my imprisonment.
Ceasing his sword-work, he is depleted:
A man has dared a god in battle.       635
Calm, I have left the house and come
Before you, taking no thought for Pentheus.

It seems to me (at least a boot sounds)
He is now out front. What will he say after this?
I'll take him easy, even if he comes in a grand rage.       640
For the wise know gentleness is wisdom.
(*Enter* PENTHEUS, *panting and exhausted.*)
    PENTHEUS. Dreadful what's happened to me. The
        stranger's
Escaped who was just now in chains.

(*trying to catch his breath*)
Uh, uh.

That's him. Why this? How do you appear       645
In front of my house? How did you get free?
    DIONYSOS. Put a calm foot, as they say, on your
        anger.
    PENTHEUS. How did you break your chains and pass
        outside?
    DIONYSOS. Did I not say, you not hear, that someone
        would set me free?
    PENTHEUS. Who? You always drag in strange words.       650

**647, Put ... anger.** The original says "under your anger."

24   *Euripides*

DIONYSOS.  He who fathers the clustering vine for
       men.
PENTHEUS.  [An evil gift to make men delirious!]
DIONYSOS.  You insulted Dionysos' glorious present!
PENTHEUS.  I order all the city gates shut!
DIONYSOS.  Why? Don't gods pass over walls?
PENTHEUS.  You are very wise, but not where you
655       should be.
DIONYSOS.  Especially there I reveal my wisdom.


But hear and learn this man's words
Who comes from the mountain to tell you something.
I'll stay for you. I won't run away.
*(A* MESSENGER *enters, stage right.)*
   MESSENGER.  Pentheus, Governor of the land of
660       Thebes,

*wordy
messenger !*

I come from Cithaeron, where the bright shafts
Of milky snow never cease.
   PENTHEUS.  What sad message do you bring?
   MESSENGER.  I saw the holy bacchants, who from our
       land
665 Flashed their milky limbs in madness.
I yearn to tell you and the city, my lord,
What horrors they perform, greater than miracles!
I want to hear if I may say freely
Those things or check my tongue.
670 I fear your quick mind, my lord,
And your temper, so kingly!
   PENTHEUS.  Speak out. You'll be safe from me.
To be angry with just men is wrong.
The more dreadful things you say of the bacchants,
675 All the more I shall punish this man
Who taught these arts to women.
   MESSENGER.  The grazing herds of cattle were just
*morning* Climbing the uplands, when the sun


**652, An evil gift . . . delirious.** This line is a later interpolation,
see "a note on the text."

Throws his rays warming the earth.
I saw three bands of dancing women,
One Autonoe led, the second
Your mother, Agaue. Ino the third.
All were sleeping, their bodies exhausted.
Some propped their backs with the thick fir branch.
Others at random had set their heads
In oak leaves on the ground, with moderation,
Not, as you say, drunk from bowl and flute,
Hunting in lonely woods for Aphrodite.

Your mother, rising in the midst of the bacchants,
Gave the cry to stir their bodies
From sleep, when she heard horned cattle lowing.
Tossing leaden sleep from their eyes,
They sprang up in formation—a miraculous sight—
Young and old with virgins still unmarried.
First they let their hair fall about their shoulders,
Fastened up their fawnskins, those whose ties
Were undone, and fastened the spotted hides
With serpents that licked their cheek.
Some, cradling deer or wolf cubs,
Offer beasts their white milk,
Whose breast still swelled for the new-borns
They abandoned. They put on ivy
Crowns, oak and fruitful bryony. *(berry vine)*
Someone struck a thyrsos on a rock,
From there water leapt out fresh.
Another let fall the fennel to the ground
And for her the god shot up a fountain of wine.
Those who longed for light drink
Scraped the ground with their fingertips,
And had milk gushing. From the ivied thyrsos
Dropped syrupy streams of honey.
So, were you there, the god you now blame,
You would approach with prayer, seeing this.

We cowherds and shepherds met together

715  Arguing about our common reports
Of their uncanny and miraculous doings.
Then some glib city vagabond
Asked us all, "You who inhabit
The revered mountain highlands, shall we chase
720  Pentheus' mother, Agaue, from the revels
And earn our lord's favor?" He seemed

*ambush for Agave ends in narrow escape*

To speak well, and we lay in wait
Camouflaged in leafy shrubs. At the set time,
They waved the thyrsos in bacchic revelling,
725  Called The God of Cries with a common tongue
And Bromios, born of Zeus. Each mountain
And Beast was possessed and set all else in motion.

Agaue happened to race by me,
And I leapt out wishing to catch her,
730  Evacuating the thicket where I hid myself.

*Agave calls for aid*

She cried out, "O my swift hounds,
We are hunted by these men, but follow,
Follow me armed with thyrsos in hand."

*witness omophagy*

Then we fled to escape being torn
735  To pieces by them. Barehanded,
They attacked cattle grazing grass.
You could see one woman drawing
Apart a young heifer, fat and bellowing,
Others tore and mangled grown heifers.
740  You could see ribs or a cloven hoof
Thrown up and down and, suspended
From fir trees, drip defiled, with blood.
Arrogant bulls too, rage once filling
Their horns, were tripped bodily to the ground,
745  Ravaged by hundreds of young hands,
And were stripped of their garment of flesh
Before you could blink your royal eyes.
They lifted off like birds under their own power,

**725, The God of Cries.** Dionysos.

Across the expanse of plain, which by Asopus'
Streams makes the rich grain for Thebes. 750
Hysiae and Erythrae, set in the uplands
Below Cithaeron, they harassed like raiders
And scattered everything topsy-turvy. ἄνω τε καὶ κάτω
Some snatched children from their homes.
They set all on their shoulders. All held 755
Without ties, and nothing fell to the black earth,
Neither bronze nor iron. They wore fire
In their hair but were unburned. The plundered
Men angrily turned to weapons,
A fearful sight to see, my lord: 760
A pointed spear did not bloody them
But *they* wounded men, letting the thyrsos
Fly from their hands. Women attacked
Men's backs in flight. Some god was there.
They drew back to where they set out, 765
To the fountains the god himself raised.
They washed their hands of blood, while serpents
Licked drops off the flesh of their cheeks.

Whoever this god is, master, welcome him
To this city. He is great in other ways: 770
He himself, I hear them say,
Gave the pain-killing vine to men.
When wine is no more, neither is love,
Nor any other pleasure for mankind.
*(Exit.)*

CHORUS. I fear to speak free words to the king, 775
But nonetheless, it shall be said:
Dionysos is inferior to no other god.
  PENTHEUS. This insolence of the bacchants is so close
    now,
It flames up like fire, a great outrage
To Greece. We can't hang back. Go 780

749–51, Asopus' . . . Hysiae . . . Erythrae. Above the valley of
the Asopus were the mountain villages of Hysiae and Erythrae.

To the Electran Gate. Call all spearmen
And all riders of swift mounts,
All the shield-bearers there are, all
Those whose hands pluck the bow-string,
785   To war on the bacchants, for this is unbearable
That we are bested by women and suffer.

    DIONYSOS. Nothing bests you, even hearing my
        words,
Pentheus. I suffered pain at your hands,
Yet I say you must not take arms against a god.
790   But be calm. Bromios won't tolerate you
Harassing the bacchants from the echoing hills.

    PENTHEUS. Will you *not* teach me, but, having broken
        jail,
Stay free? Or shall I bring justice back?

    DIONYSOS. I would sacrifice to him rather than rage
795   And kick against the whip, man to god.

    PENTHEUS. I'll sacrifice female blood, as they
        deserve,
Unleashing a spate in Cithaeron's glens.

    DIONYSOS. You will flee. To turn beaten-bronze
        shields
From the bacchic thyrsos shall be your shame.
800   PENTHEUS. I am locked with this impossible stranger,
Who neither suffering nor acting will be silent.

    DIONYSOS. It's still possible, my lord, to right things.

    PENTHEUS. By doing what? Being a slave to my
        slaves?

    DIONYSOS. I shall lead them here, with no weapons.
805   PENTHEUS. Ah! Now you plot against me!

    DIONYSOS. What plot, if I wish to save you by my
        skill?

    PENTHEUS. You made a pact so the rites would be
        eternal.

    DIONYSOS. Indeed I did, a pact with the god.

**781, Electran Gate.** The south gate of Thebes, leading to the
Cithaeron road.

PENTHEUS. *(to attendants)*  Bring my war-gear!
   *(to* DIONYSOS)                    And you be silent!
DIONYSOS. —Wait!—
Want to see them gathered in the mountains?
   PENTHEUS. *(somewhat delirious)*
—Oh yes! I would give countless gold!—
DIONYSOS. What, have you fallen so deep in love
   with them?
PENTHEUS. It would pain me to see them drunk.
DIONYSOS. Would you still see sweetly what is bitter
   for you?
PENTHEUS. Certainly, but silent, hidden under fir
   trees.
DIONYSOS. They'll track you down, even if you come
   secretly.
PENTHEUS. Openly then. You speak well.
DIONYSOS. Shall I lead you? Will you try the
   journey?
PENTHEUS. As quick as you can. I resent your delay.
DIONYSOS. Now put on a linen dress.
PENTHEUS. What? Shift myself from man to woman?
DIONYSOS. So they won't kill you, appearing as a
   man there.
PENTHEUS. Again, well said. You were wise all along.
DIONYSOS. Dionysos taught me well.
PENTHEUS. How will your sound plan be carried out?
DIONYSOS. I'll go into the house and dress you.
PENTHEUS. In what garb? A woman's? Shame
   prevents me.
DIONYSOS. You no longer desire the sight of the
   maenads?
PENTHEUS. Tell, what dress will you wrap me in?
DIONYSOS. Across your head I'll stretch a wig.
PENTHEUS. What is the second part of my costume?
DIONYSOS. A full-length robe and on your head a
   hairband.
PENTHEUS. Will you put anything else on me?
DIONYSOS. A thyrsos for your hand and a spotted
   fawnskin.

810 D.'s offer
to show
revels

P. misses
point

815

820
must
dress as
woman

825

830

835

PENTHEUS. I can't put on a woman's dress.

DIONYSOS. But you'll spill blood battling the
bacchants!

PENTHEUS. True. I must first reconnoiter.

DIONYSOS. Certainly wiser than hunting evil with
evil.

PENTHEUS. How can I pass through Cadmus' city
840    unnoticed?

DIONYSOS. We'll take lonely roads. I shall lead.

PENTHEUS. Much better, so the bacchants won't mock
me.
When we're inside,
*(coming to himself momentarily)*
                    *I'll* decide what's best.

DIONYSOS. All right. In every way, I am ready.

845  PENTHEUS. I would go, either furnished with arms
Or persuaded by your counsels.
*(Exit* PENTHEUS.*)*

DIONYSOS. Women! The man is brought into the net.
He'll come to the bacchants; there die justly.


Dionysos, It's up to you. You're not far off.
850  Let's make him pay. First set him beside
Himself in light-headed madness. Being sane,
He'll not want to wear women's robes.
His mind sidetracked, he'll put them on.
I long to make him laughingstock of the Thebans,
855  A transvestite drawn through the city,
After his earlier frightful arrogance.
But I go to put this costume on Pentheus,
The very one he will take down to hell,
Slaughtered at his mother's hands, and he'll know
860  Zeus-born Dionysos is a true divinity,
Most terrifying to men, and most kind.
*(Exit* DIONYSOS.*)*

STASIMON 3
str.

glyconic
—◆—∪∪—◦—

CHORUS.        Will I set my bare foot
                    Then in dancing vigils;
                    Rousing bacchic frenzy,

Shake my throat in dewy air,                    865
    Like a fawn in green joy
    Sporting in a meadow,
When she's fled the fearful hunt,
    Passed beyond the beaters,
        Over the woven nets,                    870
    And the shouting huntsman
Breaks off the coursing of his hounds?
She darts on across the riverside plain
    Laboring, driving, hurtling,
    Joying in the manless waste,               875
    Greenness of the forest shade.


What is wisdom? Or what lovelier gift
    From the gods, in mortal eyes,
    Than to hold a stronger hand
        Over enemy heads:
        Honor is dear—always.

*what is wisdom? (refrain; cf. 897 & 901)* 880

        Scarcely it has started,    — — — ◡ ◡ — ◡ —    *Ant.*
    Yet still god's might is trust-
    Worthy, punishes men
        Who adore ruthless force,               885
        Honor not divinities,
            In opinions mad.
    Subtle are the ways the gods
        Cover time's slow step,
        Hunting down the godless                890
    Who must know they're weaker
    Than the laws and follow custom.
For the cost is light to think *this* strength:
    That which heaven has blessed:
    What conforms in time to custom,            895
    What is born in nature, ever.


What is wisdom? Or what lovelier gift
    From the gods, in mortal eyes,

*Pentheus as woman*

32 *Euripides*

900                    Than to hold a stronger hand
                       Over enemy heads:
                       Honor is dear—always.

*Epode*                                    εὐδαίμων                    *hipponactean*
*happiness*            That man is blessed who fled the storm  ---  ∪∪–∪––
                          At sea and reached the bay.
                       And he is blessed who rose above
905                       His toil. In various ways
                       One man outstrips in wealth and power
                          Another: countless men
                       Have countless hopes: some end in joy,
                          But others drift away.
910                    The man who day to day has luck
                       In life—that man I bless.

*(Enter* DIONYSOS.*)*

EPISODE 4        DIONYSOS. Eager for what you shouldn't see,
                 Pentheus, hurrying to mischief, I'd say!
                 Come before the house. Let me look at you
915   In the dress of a woman, a maenad, a bacchant!
      A spy on your mother and her band.

*(Enter* PENTHEUS *dressed as a maenad.)*

      You look like one of Cadmus' daughters.

*Pentheus*        PENTHEUS. *(hallucinating)* Listen, I seem to see two
*hallucinates:*                                            suns,
*sees double,*   And seven-gated Thebes is double.
*sees bull*
920   A bull before me, you seem to lead the way,
      And your head has sprouted horns. Were you a beast
      All the time? Truly now you are a bull.

         DIONYSOS. The god is present, who before was
                                              unkind.
      Now he's our ally, and you see what you should.

*uncomfortable* 925  PENTHEUS. How do I look? Do I not carry myself
*humor*          Like Ino, or Agaue, my own mother?

                 DIONYSOS. Looking at you, I seem to see them.
*effeminized*    But this curl is out of place,
*Pentheus* *     Not where I tucked it under the hairband.
930              PENTHEUS. Inside waving and throwing it back

      * unlike Tetr. & Cadmus, P. loses masculinity—and thus his
      right to rule

In revelry, I unmoored it from the mitre.

DIONYSOS. Let *me* rearrange it, who wishes to serve
You. But straighten your head.

PENTHEUS. There! Dress me. I'm dedicated to you.

DIONYSOS. Your girdle is loose, and the pleats of
   your robe
Do not fall straight below the ankle.                                    935

PENTHEUS. That seems true on the right side.
On the other, my robe is straight to the tendon.

DIONYSOS. Surely you'll think me your best friend,
When you unexpectedly see the bacchants sober.                            940

PENTHEUS. Shall I appear more of a bacchant taking
The thyrsos in my right hand, or in this?

DIONYSOS. You should raise it with your right hand,
Right foot too. I commend your changed mind.

PENTHEUS. *(swelling with visions of power)* Then can
   I lift Cithaeron's glens                                              945
With those same bacchants onto my shoulders?

DIONYSOS. You can if you want. Before your mind
Was unsound. Now you think rightly.

PENTHEUS. Shall we bring crowbars? Or shall I tear
   the summits
By hand, heaving them with shoulder or arm?                              950

DIONYSOS. Come now, don't ruin the temples of the
   nymphs
And Pan's seat where he plays the pipes!

PENTHEUS. You speak well. Women should not be
   won
By strength. I'll cover my body with the fir trees.

DIONYSOS. *(aside)* You'll be covered with the cover
   you deserve,                                                          955
A crafty spy among the maenads.

PENTHEUS. Listen! I imagine them as birds in the
   undergrowth,
Clenched in the most delightful nets of love-making.


**952, Pan.** A god of flocks and shepherds, whose appearance
caused "panic" among travellers.

Dionysos. Indeed. For that you are sent as a
watcher.

Perhaps you'll take them,

960 *(aside)* if they don't take you first.

Pentheus. Escort me through the middle of Thebes.
I alone of these men dare this!

*irony of P's experience*

Dionysos. You alone labor for the city,
So struggles await you, long overdue.

965 Follow me, your guard and deliverer. There
Another leads you. *sc. brings you back*

Pentheus. She who bore me.

Dionysos. A sign to all.

Pentheus. I go for that.

Dionysos. You'll ride back.

Pentheus. You speak of luxury.

Dionysos. In mother's hands.

Pentheus. You promise me to spoil me.

Dionysos. Spoiling in my way.

970 Pentheus. I'll take what's due.

Dionysos. Terrible you are, and come to terrible
suffering, δεινὸς σὺ δεινὸς κἀπὶ δείν' ἔρχει πάθη
So you'll discover fame lifted to heaven.

*(aside)*

Stretch your hands, Agaue and you daughters
Sprung from Cadmus. I bring a youngster

975 To this great contest. I shall be the victor,
And Bromios, as events will show.

*(They go out.)*

υυυ—–—υυυ—υ—

*Stasimon 4 Str.*

Chorus. Go swift hell-hounds of Lyssa, to
The mountain where the nymphs of Cadmus
Gather their bands. Lash them to madness

980 Against the manic maenad spy
In womanish disguise.
His mother first will spot him

---

**977, Lyssa.** "Canine madness." Personified, she is a goddess of
madness who hunts with hell-hounds.

Spying from some sheer rock or peak
And rouse the maenads:
"What son of Cadmus, O Bacchants,    985
Has come into the mountain— ‿‿‿ ‿‿‿ ‿‿‿ ‑‑‑ *
*Has come into the mountain!—*
A seeker of the mountain-runners.
What creature bore him? Not from human blood
He sprang but from some lioness
Or race of Libyan Gorgons."    990

ἴτω δίκα φανερός, ἴτω ξιφηφόρος

Let Justice walk bright, let her bear a sword,   *refrain (cf. 877 ff.)*
Hacking the throat of Echion's child,
The godless, mindless, unjust man of earth.   995

The man who starts with unjust mind ‿‿‿ ‑‑‑ ‿‿‿ ‑‑‑ *  *Ant.*
And lawless rage against your rites,
O Bacchos, and your mother's,
His mind deranged, his will crazed   1000
To beat the Masterless,
Unhesitating death
Will moderate his mind on gods.
To live a mortal
Life is painless. I grudge no wisdom   1005
And joy in its pursuit,
But other greatness gleams:
O would life flow to beauty, day
Through night, and one be pure and reverent,
Casting away the unjust custom,
To magnify the gods.   1010

Let Justice walk bright, let her bear a sword,
Hacking the throat of Echion's child,
The godless, mindless, unjust man of earth.   1015

Appear a bull, a many-headed   *Epode bull, snake, lion*
Dragon, or blazing lion.

**990, Gorgons.** Three female monsters with snakes for hair.

* resolved anap.? ‿‿ ⏑̆ ‿‿ ⏑̆ ‿‿‑ ‿̄ ‑

36  *Euripides*

1020

Come, Bacchos, with your smiling face,
And toss the fatal rope
About the hunter of the bacchants—
Who fell among the maenads.

(SECOND MESSENGER *enters.*)

EPISODE 5

SECOND MESSENGER. O House, once fortunate
throughout Greece,

1025 Born of the old Sidonian who sowed the earth-born
Crop of the dragon in the serpent's land,
How I grieve for you, though but a slave.

CHORUS.                What is it?
What news of the bacchants do you disclose?

P. is dead 1030 MESSENGER. Pentheus is destroyed, Child of Echion.

CHORUS.
Great Bromios, you are revealed a god!

MESSENGER. What do you say? What have you said?
You women joy in my master's misfortunes?

CHORUS.      A stranger crying "Evoe"
In my bacchic songs,

1035          I crouch no more in fear of chains.

MESSENGER. You think Thebes so manless . . .

CHORUS.      It's Dionysos, Dionysos, he,
Not Thebes, wields power over me!

MESSENGER. It is excusable, but not right,

1040 To rejoice, women, after misfortunes.

CHORUS.
Will you speak and show me by what fate he died,
The unjust man, contriver of injustice?

MESSENGER. After we left the rural outskirts
Of Thebes, we crossed Asopus' streams

1045 And entered the hill country of Cithaeron,

P.'s death   Pentheus and I, me following my master,
And the stranger who was leader of our expedition.

First we sat in a grassy opening,
Holding silent both foot and tongue,

1050 So we would see and not be seen.

**1025, Sidonian.** For Sidon, see note to line 172.
**1044, Asopus' streams.** See note to lines 749–51.

There was a well-watered gully, surrounded by cliffs,
Deep-shaded with pine, where the maenads
Sat, employed in delightful toil.
Some, laying aside the thyrsos,
Crowned its hair again with ivy.                    1055
Free as fillies of the embroidered yoke,
Others chanted bacchic antiphons.
Poor Pentheus, not seeing the company
Of women, said, "Stranger, where we stand,
My eyes don't reach the pseudo-maenads.             1060
But on the slopes, up a towering fir,
I would see clearly maenad obscenities."

Then, I saw the stranger's miracle:
Grasping a fir branch high as heaven,
He brought it down, down, down to the black earth,  1065
Circled like a bow, or as a rounded wheel
Rotates its course, being chalked for a rim.
So the stranger's hands curved the mountain
Stem to earth, a deed not mortal.
Making Pentheus sit on the fir branches,            1070
He released the shoot straight up through his hands
Without shaking, taking care lest it throw him.
Steep in the steep heaven it was lifted,
Holding my master seated on its back.
But he was seen, rather than saw the maenads.       1075
He was barely visible, seated high,
And the stranger no longer there,
When, from the air, a voice,
Like Dionysos' roared out, "O maidens,
I bring the man who made you                         1080
And me and our rites a laughingstock.
Take vengeance." And as he spoke, a light
Of holy fire stood between heaven and earth.

The air was silent. The silent valley held
Its leaves. You heard no animal cry.                1085
Not hearing the sound clearly,

They stood up and gazed around.
He called out again. When Cadmus daughters
Recognized Bacchos' clear command,
1090 They darted, with no less speed than doves,
Their running feet driven by violence,
His mother Agaue and her siblings,
And all the bacchants. Through torrent, gorge,
Crag, they leapt frantic with the god's breath.
1095 When they saw my master seated on the fir,
They first hurled murderous stones
At him, mounting a towering rock,
And pine branches struck at him.
Others cast the thyrsos through the air
1100 At Pentheus—horrible thrusts—but they failed.
Holding a height higher than their rage,
My master sat wretched, a trapped captive.
Then, like lightning they shattered oak branches
And plucked at roots with wooden crowbars.
1105 When they could not achieve their end,
Agaue said, "Come, form a ring,
Maenads. Grasp the trunk so we may take
The treed beast, lest he report
God's secret dances." They set
uproot tree 1110 A thousand hands to the fir-tree, rooted it
From the ground. Seated high, from high
Down to earth, crying, crying, fell
Pentheus, who learned destruction was near.

First Agaue, priestess of the kill, began
1115 And fell upon him. He stripped his mitre
From his head, so poor Agaue would know
his pleas        And not kill him, and said touching
Her cheek, "It's me, mother, your child
Pentheus, whom you bore in Echion's house.
1120 Pity me, mother, don't murder
Me, your son, for my sins!"

Coughing foam and casting about

Her deranged gaze, mindless where she should be
    mindful,
Possessed of Bacchos and unpersuaded by Pentheus,    *dismember-*
Seizing his left forearm, bracing    1125 *ment*
Her foot in the ribs of the doomed man,
She ripped out the shoulder. Not by her strength,
But the god put skill in her hands.
Ino ruined the other side,
Breaking the flesh, and Autonoe and the whole mob    1130
Of Bacchants attacked, all one shout:
While he groaned with all his breath,
They screamed triumph. One carried off a forearm,
Another a foot still booted. His ribs
Were raked bare. Each bloodied her hands    1135
Playing catch with Pentheus' flesh.

The body lies scattered: part beneath
Rough rocks, the rest in deep-forest foliage,
Not easily found. The sad head,
Which his mother happened to seize by hand,    1140
She fixed on the top of her thyrsos, as it were    *head on*
A mountain lion's she bore through Cithaeron,    *thyrsus*
Leaving her sisters in bacchic dance.
She comes within these walls, exulting
In her ill-starred beast, calling Bacchos    1145
Her "Fellow Hunter," "Helper in the Kill,"
"Giver of Victory," for whom she wins tears.

Now I go far from this disaster
Before Agaue arrives home.
To be moderate and honor godly things    1150
Is best. I think it the wisest possession
For mortal men, if they use it well.
*(Exit.)*

   CHORUS.   Let's celebrate the bacchic god. ∨∨∨ – – – – ∨∨    *STASIMON 5*
                     Let's cry aloud the doom that fell
                        On Pentheus, the Dragon's child,    1155

Who took a woman's robe and reed
Made to a thyrsos—certain death.
A bull led him to his downfall.

1160   Cadmeian bacchants, you have changed
The victory song to woe, to tears.
A lovely game—
To clothe a dripping hand in one's son's blood.

EXODOS

1165   But, I see Pentheus' mother, Agaue,     *quasi-kommos (lyric interlude)*
Rushing to the house with distracted eyes.
Receive the revel of the bacchic god!
*(Enter* AGAUE *with the head of* PENTHEUS.)

Str.

AGAUE.   Asian Bacchants!
CHORUS.                         O, why force me?
AGAUE.   From the mountains I carry home
1170                         Tendrils fresh cut.
                              Blessed hunting.
CHORUS.
              Yes. I welcome you a fellow reveller.
AGAUE.             Without nets I seized this
                    New-born son of a killer lion,
1175                         As you can see.
CHORUS.                 In what desert?
AGAUE.   Cithaeron.
CHORUS.                 Yes, Cithaeron?
AGAUE.             Cithaeron has killed him.
CHORUS.   Who struck him down?
AGAUE.                                      Mine's the honor
                                              first.
1180   Blessed Agaue I'm called by the reverent.
CHORUS.   Who else?
AGAUE.                         Cadmus' . . .
CHORUS.   Cadmus' what?
AGAUE.                         Race.
              After me, they touched this wild beast.
              After me! This hunt was lucky.

Share now the feast.                                    *Ant.*

CHORUS.                          What? Share? Poor girl!
AGAUE.
    The young bull just sprouts down upon          1185
          His chin, under
          The soft hair crest.
CHORUS. Yes, its hair is like a savage beast's.
AGAUE.          Bacchos, the wise hunter,
      Wisely drove his maenads after                  1190
        This wild creature.
CHORUS.              Hunter Bacchos!
AGAUE.          Do you praise me?
CHORUS.                              Yes, I praise you.
AGAUE.      Soon the Cadmeians will—
CHORUS.  Pentheus too your child—
AGAUE.                              Will praise his mother 1195
    Bringing down this lion-hearted quarry.
CHORUS.          Strange spoil.
AGAUE.                          Strange hunt.
CHORUS.              Proud?
AGAUE.                      I'm joyous.
      In this hunt I brought about
      Great things—great things are manifest!
CHORUS.  Then reveal to the citizens, wretched
  woman,                                   *iambics*          1200
The prize-winning quarry you come bringing.
  AGAUE.  O you who live in Thebes, the town
Of beautiful towers, come see this catch,
The beast which we daughters of Cadmus took,
Not with the thonged spears of Thessaly,               1205
Or with nets, but with the white blades
Of our fingers. So should anyone boast
Of using the spearmakers' needless weapons?
With *this* hand, we seized the animal
And scattered its limbs to the winds.                  1210

Where is my old father? Let him come near.             *where is
Cadmus?*

**1205, Thessaly.** A region of northern Greece.

*Cadmus with body* (handwritten margin note, top)

*where is Pentheus?* (handwritten margin note)

And where is my son, Pentheus? Let him take it,
Climbing the ladder in front of the house.
So he may pin to the frieze the head
1215 Of this lion I come bringing from the hunt.
(*Enter* Cadmus *and his train bringing the remains of*
      Pentheus.)
 Cadmus. Follow me and set the sad weight

*reassembled body of P.* (handwritten margin note)

Of Pentheus before his house, my men,
Whose body I bear, wearied after much searching,
Discovering it scattered in the glens of Cithaeron,
1220 Gathering nothing in the same place,
But lying in woods hard to penetrate.


I heard of the recklessness of my daughters,
As I entered the city walls
From the revels with old Teiresias.
1225 Turning back to the mountain,
I retrieved her child slaughtered by maenads.
I saw Autonoe, who bore Actaeon
To Aristaeus, and Ino together, still
About the thickets in their sad madness.
1230 Someone said Agaue had come here
In bacchic dance, nor did I hear wrong.
I look on her now—a cursed sight.
 Agaue. Father, You can make the greatest boast:
You have fathered the best daughters by far
1235 Of all men, the greatest, and me above the others.
Leaving the shuttle by the loom, I have come
To greater things: taking a beast by hand.
I bear it in my arms, as you see,
Winning this prize of honor to hang
1240 Before your house. Receive it, Father,
In your hands. Proud of my hunt,
Call your friends to the feast, for you are blest,
Blest, in our accomplishing great things!

*Cadmus views crime* (handwritten margin note)

 Cadmus. O sorrow, immeasurable and unsightly,
1245 Accomplishing murder with your wretched hands.

Casting down a noble victim for the gods,
You invite our Thebes and me to the feast.
O, your troubles first, then mine!
How the god destroyed us justly, but too much,
Lord Bromios, one of our own family.

*D.'s just
punishment*

1250

AGAUE. How hard to please is old age
And sullen-faced. Would my son were lucky
In hunting, following his mother's ways,
When he hunts with the Theban youth!
But being what he is, he only fights
The gods. You should scold him, father.
Who would call him here to my sight
So he may witness my good fortune?

1255

CADMUS. Oh no, no! Knowing what you have done,
You will suffer horribly. If you remain to the end
Always in the state you are in now,
Being unfortunate, you will seem uncursed.

1260

AGAUE. What here is unseemly or painful?
CADMUS. Set your eyes first on that sky.
AGAUE. There. But why advise me to look?
CADMUS. Does it seem to you the same or to
change?

1265

AGAUE. Brighter and more lucid than before.
CADMUS. Is your soul still distracted?
AGAUE. I don't understand. Somehow, I'm
turning . . .

*Agave
regains
senses*

Sane, setting aside my earlier thoughts.

1270

CADMUS. Will you hear something and answer
clearly?
AGAUE. Indeed, I forgot what we just said, father.
CADMUS. Into what house did you come singing the
bridal song?
AGAUE. You gave me to Echion, the Dragon's child,
they say.
CADMUS. What child was born at home to your
husband?

1275

AGAUE. Pentheus, from my union with his father.
CADMUS. Whose face do you hold in your arms?

AGAUE. A lion's. . . . So the huntresses told me.

CADMUS. Look straight now. Seeing takes little effort.

*Agave*
*recognizes*
*head* 1280

AGAUE. —Ahh!—

What do I see? What do I carry in my hands?

CADMUS. Observe and learn more clearly.

AGAUE. Poor me! I see the greatest sorrow in the
world.

CADMUS. Does it seem to you to look like a lion?

AGAUE. No! No! But pitiful! I hold Pentheus' head.

1285  CADMUS. Wept for before you recognized him.

AGAUE. Who killed him? How did he come to my
hands?

CADMUS. Truth is a curse. How it comes at the
wrong time!

AGAUE. Say it! My heart jumps at what's to come.

CADMUS. *You* killed him, and your sisters.

1290  AGAUE. Where? At home or in what place?

CADMUS. The very place where the dogs divided
Actaeon.

AGAUE. Why did the unlucky man come to
Cithaeron?

CADMUS. He went to mock the god and your revels.

AGAUE. How did *we* land there?

CADMUS. You were mad. The whole city went mad
1295   with Bacchos.  Διόνυσος ἡμᾶς ὤλεσ'ὸ, ἄρτι μανθάνω.

*D. has*
*destroyed*
*us all*

AGAUE. Dionysos has destroyed us. I know that now.

ὕβριν ὁβρισθείς
CADMUS. Run amok with insult, for you denied him.

*Cadmus notes*
*her crime*

AGAUE. Where is my beloved son's body, Father?

CADMUS. I have it after careful searching.

1300  AGAUE. Are its limbs set well together?

What did my madness have to do with Pentheus?

CADMUS. You turned out like him, ⌐not honoring the
god,⌐

Who linked you all in one calamity,

This boy too, so our house is ruined

*Cadmus* 1305
*is ruined*
*also*

And me, who am childless of male offspring.

I see, poor woman, the fruit of your womb

*Dionysus returns, divine (theophany)* [handwritten annotation]

Most foully and horribly murdered,
He who revived our house.
*(turning toward* PENTHEUS' *body)*
                You, child, who held
My family together, child of my child,
Were a terror to the city, but no one       1310
Dared insult the old man before you,
For he would suffer a proper punishment.
Now dishonored, I shall be driven from home,    *Cadmus must go* [handwritten]
The great Cadmus, who sowed the race
Of Thebes and reaped the most noble crop.     1315
O most beloved of men—though no longer alive,
Child, still you will be counted among my beloved—
No longer touching this chin with your hand,
Will you greet and hug your mother's father, child,
Saying, "Who treats you wrong, dishonors you, old
     one?                                 1320
What troublemaker shakes your heart?
Tell, then I shall chastise your wrongdoer, father."
~~[lacuna *]~~
Now I am miserable, and you wretched,
A pitiable mother with sorrowing sisters.
If there is anyone who despises the gods,     *! believe!* [handwritten] 1325
Looking on this death, let him believe.

     CHORUS. I suffer for you, Cadmus. Your grandson    *P.'s just death* [handwritten]
Had a just punishment, but you pain.

     AGAVE. Father, you see how my life is perverted!    *< lacuna*** [handwritten]
*(Enter* DIONYSOS *from above.)*

     DIONYSOS. You will be changed to a serpent, and    *Cadmus' future* [handwritten]
     your wife                             1330
Turning wild will assume a snake's body,
Harmonia, whom you, a mortal, took from Ares.
With your wife, you shall drive a chariot of bullocks

---

**1329ff, Father … perverted.** Some lines are probably missing
after this line. The prediction of changing Cadmus and Harmonia
into snakes who lead a barbarian army against Greece and then
go to the Land of the Blest is obscure in origin and meaning.
See Dodds' commentary on these lines.

\* *Agave's lament; Chorus announces Dionysus; Dionysus tells of Pentheus'*
*Agave's & sister's, and Cadmus' punishments.* [handwritten footnote]

And lead barbarians, according to the oracle of Zeus.

1335 With an innumerable force, you shall lay waste
Many cities, and when they plunder the oracle
Of Apollo, they shall have a painful trip back,
But Ares will rescue you and Harmonia
And will set you, living, in the Land of the Blest.

*Cad. & Harm. will be rewarded by Ares*

1340 I speak this, Dionysos, descended from
No mortal father, but from Zeus. If you knew
How to be wise, when you would not,
Happy, you would have Zeus' son for ally.

CADMUS. Dionysos, we beg you. We did wrong.

*we have sinned*

DIONYSOS. Too late* you know me. When you should

*too late* 1345   have, you did not. ἔγνώ καμεν ταῦτα· ἀλλ' ἐπεξέρχει λίαν.

*we have learned*

CADMUS. We know now—but you overpunish!

DIONYSOS. A god, I suffered outrage at your hands!

CADMUS. It is not right the gods resemble men in
anger.

DIONYSOS. My father Zeus approved this long ago.

1350 AGAUE. O, old man, painful exile is decreed.

DIONYSOS. Why delay what must be so? εἰς δεινὸν ... κακόν

CADMUS. How we all have come to terrible harm,
Child, sad you and your sisters,
And wretched me. An old exile

1355 I go to some barbarians. The oracle adds
I am to lead a motley army against Greece.
My wife, Harmonia, Ares' child,
Taking on the savage form of snake,
A snake myself, I'll assault altars

1360 And Greek tombs, commanding spearmen.
Wrecked by evil, I shall not stop suffering:
Not even when I sail down to hell shall I be calm.

AGAUE. O Father, losing you, I'll be an exile.

CADMUS. Why do you hug me, poor child,

1365 Like a young swan hugs one weak and white?

AGAUE. But cast off, where shall I turn?

CADMUS. I don't know, child. A father, I'm little
help.

*cF. Ant. 1270: οἴμ' ὡς ἔοικας ὀψὲ τὴν δίκην ἰδεῖν

χαῖρ', ὦ μέλαθρον, χαῖρ', ὦ πατρίᾳ
——‿ ‿‿— ——‿‿—

AGAUE.

Goodbye, my house. Goodbye, my native city. *anapaestic*
    I leave you in misfortune, *Agave banished*
      Fleeing my bridal chambers. 1370

CADMUS. Depart now, child, to Aristaeus'.

AGAUE. I cry for you, Father.

CADMUS.                And I for you, Child,
    I weep too for your sisters.

AGAUE.       Lord Dionysos brought 1375
    This frightful torture on your house.

DIONYSOS.

    I suffered frightful things from you,
    My name dishonored in Thebes!

AGAUE.      Farewell, my father.

CADMUS.          My poor daughter, farewell—
    Though hardly will you "fare well." 1380

AGAUE.

    Lead me, my friends, so we may gather *Agave wants to escape Dionysioca*
    My miserable sisters in exile.
      May I go where
    Bloodied Cithaeron sees me not,
    Nor I Cithaeron with my eyes, 1385
     Nor where the memory
    Is dedicated to the thyrsos—
  Leave them a care to other bacchants.

CHORUS.    Divinity takes many forms. *cf. finale of Helen*
The gods accomplish many things beyond all hope.
    What is expected is not brought to pass. 1390
      But god discovers means
    To bring about the unexpected:
      Such was the outcome here. τοιόνδε ἀπέβη τόδε πρᾶγμα

*(All go out.)*

---

**1371, Aristaeus.** Aristaeus was her brother-in-law, husband of Autonoe. See "introduction."

# The Frogs

# Aristophanes

# Characters

XANTHIAS, *slave of Dionysos*
DIONYSOS, *the god, also called Iacchos and Bacchos*
HERACLES *(Hercules)*
CORPSE
CHARON, *ferryman of the dead*
CHORUS OF FROGS *(offstage)*
CHORUS OF INITIATES, *followers of Dionysos*
AEACUS, *gatekeeper of Hades*
SERVANT OF PERSEPHONE, *queen of Hades*
HOSTESS OF AN INN
COOKIE, *her servant*
SERVANT OF PLUTO
EURIPIDES, *the tragedian*
AESCHYLUS, *the tragedian*
PLUTO, *God of Hades*
PALLBEARERS, TWO ATTENDANTS OF AEACUS, MUSE OF EURI-
    PIDES *(silent parts)*

Ἀριστοφάνους Βάτραχοι

*(Scene: Stage center is a house with a door. DIONYSOS enters, wearing, over his yellow tunic, HERACLES' lion-skin and carrying HERACLES' great club. XANTHIAS enters, carrying baggage on a pole over his shoulder and riding a donkey.)*

trimeters
1–207

XANTHIAS.  Shall I say one of the usual things,
my lord, the spectators always laugh at?*

PROLOGUE

DIONYSOS.  By Zeus, what you like, but not "I'm hard-
    pressed,"

*(squatting down)*

not that. It's really disgusting now.

XANTHIAS.  Not some other quip?

DIONYSOS.                          Except "I'm tight-squeezed."  5

XANTHIAS.  Well, shall I say the really funny one?

DIONYSOS.  Be bold, but not that one, by Zeus!

XANTHIAS.                                        Which?

DIONYSOS.  That, shifting your pole, you want to poop.

scatology

XANTHIAS.  Nor that hauling this load,
if no one takes it, I'll bust out?                        10

DIONYSOS.  No, please, only when I'm going to vomit.

XANTHIAS.  Why then must I lug these bags,
if I don't make any of the jokes Phrynichus
was accustomed to make and Lycis and Ameipsias,
when they carried baggage in their comedies?             15

DIONYSOS.  Don't do it now! When I am in the
    audience — *i.e., as the statue of Dionysus*
and note any of this old wit,
I leave the theater, years older.    *( i.e., annual festival )*

XANTHIAS.  O, thrice-damned is this neck,
tight-squeezed and can't joke!                           20

DIONYSOS.  Isn't this pride and great insolence,
when I, Dionysos, Son of Jug, υἱὸς Σταμνίου
walk and labor and let him ride,
so he won't suffer and carry a load!

XANTHIAS.  I don't carry a load?

DIONYSOS.                          How can you if you're carried?  25

**14–15, Phrynichus . . . Lycis . . . Ameipsias.** Three writers of comedy whose works have perished.

\* *iambic trim. rendered as iambic pent.*

51

52   *Aristophanes*

XANTHIAS. Carrying *this*.
DIONYSOS.                       How?
XANTHIAS.                              Under pressure.
DIONYSOS.  Isn't your load carried by the donkey?
XANTHIAS.  Not what *I* carry, by Zeus, no!
DIONYSOS.  How can you carry, being carried by
    another?
XANTHIAS.  I don't know, but my shoulder's "hard-
30    pressed."
DIONYSOS.  OK, since you claim the donkey doesn't
    help,
change: pick up and carry the donkey.

*Arginusae*

XANTHIAS.  Damn, why didn't I fight at sea?
A free man, I'd wish you good . . . grief.
35    DIONYSOS.  Down, rogue, I'm already walking
near the door I wanted first
to go in.
            Servant, I say, boy!

*Herades*

*(Enter* HERACLES.*)*
HERACLES.  Who's beating the door? He leaps on it
like a centaur. . . . What is it? Speak!
DIONYSOS.  My boy!
XANTHIAS.            What is it?
DIONYSOS.                        Didn't you notice?
40    XANTHIAS.                                    What?
DIONYSOS.  How he fears me.
XANTHIAS.                    By Zeus, fears your madness.
HERACLES.  By Demeter, how can I not laugh?
I bite my lip, and I laugh anyway.
DIONYSOS.  My good man, come here. I need
    something from you.
45    HERACLES.  But I can't choke my laughter,
seeing a lion-skin lying on a yellow robe.
What's your game? Why come with boot and club?
Where on earth have you been?

**33, fight at sea.** Athens freed the slaves who fought at the Battle
of Arginusae in 406 B.C. *—off coast of Mytilene*

DIONYSOS.                    Under Cleisthenes.              *(effeminate)*
HERACLES.  Serving at sea?
DIONYSOS.                    We downed twelve
or thirteen of the enemies' ships.                                    50
HERACLES.  You two?
DIONYSOS.              By Apollo!
XANTHIAS. *(aside)*              Then I woke up.
DIONYSOS.  In fact while at sea reading
Euripides' *Andromeda*, I was racked
by a desire so strong you can't imagine.
HERACLES.  A desire? How big?
DIONYSOS.                    Small as Big Molon!      55
HERACLES.  For a woman?
DIONYSOS.              Oh no!
HERACLES.              Then a boy?
DIONYSOS.                        Not at all.
HERACLES.  A man then?
DIONYSOS.              Aaaah!
HERACLES.                    Did you contact
                            Cleisthenes?
DIONYSOS.  Don't mock me, O brother, I'm in a bad
   way;
such longing undoes me.
HERACLES.  What, little brother?
DIONYSOS.                    I can't say,              60
But I'll tell you through riddle.
Have you ever had a desire for pea soup?
HERACLES.  Pea soup, my god, a thousand times.
DIONYSOS.  Clear, or shall I speak another way?
HERACLES.  Not about pea soup. I know it well.        65
DIONYSOS.  A like desire consumes me for—
Euripides.
HERACLES.    Even when he's dead!

*Dionysus wants Euripides*

49, **Cleisthenes.** A notorious Athenian, mocked in several of Aristophanes' plays.
53, **Euripides' *Andromeda*.** A romantic play of longing, by Euripides, now lost.
55, **Big Molon.** A hugh actor in Euripides' plays?

DIONYSOS.  No man could persuade me
not to find him.

    HERACLES.      Even in Hell?

70    DIONYSOS.  By Zeus, I'd go even lower.

    HERACLES.  Why?

    DIONYSOS.          I want a skillful poet
    "They are no longer here; those here are base."

    HERACLES.  Doesn't Sophocles' son yet live?

    DIONYSOS.                              He's the only
good thing that's left, if he *is* good,

75 and I'm not sure that he is.

    HERACLES.  Aren't you going to raise Sophocles?
He's better than Euripides, if you must.

    DIONYSOS.  No, I'll assay the son's metal
by taking him alone, without father.

80 Besides Euripides is rogue enough
to slip back here for me.
The other one's as happy there as here.

    HERACLES.  Where's Agathon?

    DIONYSOS.                      Left me and departed.
A good poet lamented by his friends.

    HERACLES.  Where is the poor bugger?

85    DIONYSOS.                          At the Feast of the Blest.

    HERACLES.  And Xenocles?

    DIONYSOS                  Let him die, by Zeus.

    HERACLES.  And Pythangelus?

(DIONYSOS *gives a gesture of contempt.*)

    XANTHIAS. *(aside)*            Not a word about me,
flaying my shoulder like this.

    HERACLES.  Aren't there those other sissies around here

90 who carpenter more than a thousand tragedies
and out-filibuster Euripides by a mile?

    DIONYSOS.  Grape leaves and mouthwork,

---

**72, "They . . . here."** An allusion to Euripides' lost *Oineus*.
**73, Sophocles' son.** Iophron reportedly wrote fifty tragedies.
**83, Agathon.** A famous tragedian, who, like Euripides, went to the
sumptuous court of Agelaus in Macedonia. See line 85.
**86-7, Xenocles . . . Pythangelus.** Hack tragic poets.

choirs of swallows and breakers of art,
who scoot fast if they get one chorus,
and make one quick piss on tragedy.
Look and you won't find one fertile poet
who could recite a noble phrase.

HERACLES. Fertile? πῶς γόνιμον;
DIONYSOS        Fertile—one who will
utter something audacious like
"Air, Zeus' cottage," or "The foot of Time"
or "A mind that would not swear at sacrifice;
A tongue that broke an oath outside the mind."

HERACLES. You like that?
DIONYSOS.                I'm more than mad about it.
HERACLES. By God, they're jokes—you *know* it too.
DIONYSOS. Don't manage *my* mind. Stay home!
HERACLES. Also they seem artless and totally corrupt.
DIONYSOS. *You* just teach me to feast.
XANTHIAS. *(aside)*           Not a word about me.

DIONYSOS. But this is why I came in costume,
in your very image—so you may tell
me your hosts, if I need them,
the time you went after Cerberus.
Tell me those harbors, bakeries,
brothels, inns, by-ways, fountains,
roads, cities, boarding-houses, hostesses,
where the fewest bedbugs are.

XANTHIAS. *(aside)*           Not a word about me.
HERACLES. O tireless heart, do you dare it, even you?
DIONYSOS. No more of this, but tell us the quickest
road we can take to the underworld,
one that's not too cold or hot.

HERACLES. Well then, what shall I tell you first?
One way is with rope and bench—
by hanging yourself.

*marginalia:* 95 no one with staying power or depth

*marginalia:* 100

*marginalia:* 105

*marginalia:* D. wants travel tips as he 110 retraces Heracles' route as Heracles

*marginalia:* 115

*marginalia:* 120 how to go to hell

---

**100–02, "Air . . . mind."** The first phrase alludes to Euripides' lost
*Melanippe.* The second is from his *Bacchae* (l. 888). The third
alludes to his *Hippolytus* (612).
**111, Cerberus.** The three-headed guard dog of Hades.

DIONYSOS.          Stop. Too stifling.

HERACLES.   There's the well-trodden short cut,
the one through mortar.

*take hemlock*

DIONYSOS.               You mean hemlock?

HERACLES.   Of course.

125   DIONYSOS.               Too stiff, and wintry.
For your shins begin to freeze at once.

HERACLES.   Want a quick one? Straight down?

DIONYSOS.   Walking, by Zeus, is not my art.

HERACLES.   Then *creep* down to Cerameicus.

DIONYSOS.                              Then what?

HERACLES.   Going up the high tower—

130   DIONYSOS.                         What do I do?

HERACLES.   From there, watch the torch race start,
and, when the spectators cry "Let 'em go,"
let yourself go.

DIONYSOS.   Where?

HERACLES.          Down.

DIONYSOS.   But I'd break my double-brain pancake.
I won't walk that road.

135   HERACLES.          What then?

DIONYSOS.   The one *you* used.

HERACLES.                   That sailing is grueling.
Right off, you come to a lake, huge
and bottomless.

DIONYSOS.      Then how do I cross?

*ferryman's fee*

HERACLES.   In a boatling, this tiny, an old man
140   carries you, charging ⌞two obols.⌟   *cf. two obols admission to Theater*

DIONYSOS.   Whoa!   *usually one obol*
How far two obols can get you—everywhere!
How did they get down there?

HERACLES.                   Theseus brought them.
After, you see serpents and thousands of ogres
—real horrors.

**129, Cerameicus.** A luxurious suburb of Athens. From a tower
there, the torch race, dedicated to Athena, was visible.

**142, Theseus.** According to myth, the Athenian hero, Theseus, had
descended to Hades.

DIONYSOS.   Don't shock and scare me.
You won't turn me back.

HERACLES.                And all the slime,                    145
and ever-flowing dung; those lying in it,
anyone who ever wronged a guest,
or buggered a boy and filched back the money,
or thrashed mother, or rapped father's
jaw, or swore a forsworn oath,                                150
or anyone who used a speech of Morsimus.

DIONYSOS.  By the gods it was a requirement too
for anyone who learned Cinesias' war-dance.

HERACLES.  There, a blowing of flutes surrounds you.
You'll see the brightest light, like here,        155 Dionysian-
myrtle clumps and blessed choruses                    Eleusinian
of men, women, and a great clapping of hands.          Initiates

DIONYSOS.  And who *are* these?

HERACLES.                    The Initiated.

XANTHIAS. *(aside)* Then by Zeus, I'm the donkey of
    the Mysteries.
But I won't hold these things any longer.                    160

HERACLES.  They'll recite in chorus what you need,
for they dwell beside that very road,
at the doors of Pluto's Hell.
Fare thee well, Brother.

DIONYSOS.            By Zeus, you
stay fit.

*(Exit* HERACLES.*)* Take the bedding up again!              165

XANTHIAS.  Even before it's set down?

DIONYSOS.                    And very quickly too.

XANTHIAS.  No, I beg you, just hire anyone
being carted down here for the job.

DIONYSOS.  If I don't find one?

XANTHIAS.            Take me.

DIONYSOS.                Well said.

---

**151, Morsimus.** A hack tragedian and grand nephew of Aeschylus.
**153, Cinesias.** A wiry, lyric poet.
**158, The Initiated.** Male and female followers of Dionysos, who
have been initiated into his mysteries.

58   *Aristophanes*

(CORPSE *enters carried by pallbearers.*)

170   In fact they're carrying some corpse right now.

You there! I mean you, dead man!
You sir? Want to carry a little luggage?

CORPSE.  How much?
DIONYSOS.                    These here.
CORPSE.                              Will you pay two drachma?
DIONYSOS.  No, by Zeus, less.
CORPSE. (*to his pallbearers*)  Go on, down the road!
DIONYSOS.  Wait, my friend. Perhaps I can deal.
CORPSE.  If you won't plunk down two drachma, forget
   it.
DIONYSOS.  Take one-and-a-half.
CORPSE.                    Hell, I'd rather be alive again.

(CORPSE *is carried off.*)

DIONYSOS.  How stuck-up the rotter is! Won't he drop
   dead?
XANTHIAS.  I'll plod on.
DIONYSOS.                    *You* are reliable and kind.
Let's go to the boat.

(*Enter* CHARON *in his boat.*)

180   CHARON.                    Easy now. Lay her in.
XANTHIAS.  What's this?
DIONYSOS.                    This? A lake, by Zeus,
The one he mentioned, and I see a boat.
XANTHIAS.  By Poseidon, that's the real Charon!
DIONYSOS.  Charon, greetings! Greetings, Charon!
CHARON.  Anyone for a stopover from pain and
185      business?
Anyone for the Plain of Forgetfulness, for Donkey-Hair,
for Hell-Hounds, for the Crows, or the Spartan coast?
DIONYSOS.  Me!
CHARON.        Board quickly.

---

**186–87, Anyone . . . coast.** The Plain of Forgetfulness later became
the River Lethe. "Donkey-Hair" suggests "Noplace." To "go to
the crows!" meant "Drop dead!" The Spartan coast was dangerous
because of the war.

DIONYSOS.                    Where do you put in—
into Crows really?

CHARON.        By Zeus, just for you.
Get in.

DIONYSOS.  Here, boy.

CHARON.                I carry no slave,                    190
unless he fought in the save-your-ass seafight.

XANTHIAS.  Not me. I contracted eye trouble.

CHARON.  *Surely* you'll circle about the lake?

XANTHIAS.  Where shall I wait?

CHARON.                    By the Withering Stone
at the Repose Inn.

DIONYSOS.        Understand?

XANTHIAS.                    Too well.                    195
I'm double-damned! What crossed my path?
*(Exit* XANTHIAS.*)* ἐπὶ κώπην

CHARON.  Take the oar! If anyone's sailing, hurry up!
What are you *doing*?

DIONYSOS.  ἐπὶ κώπης  Me? Nothing
but sitting on the oar, as you ordered.

CHARON.  *Surely* you'll sit there, Mr. Paunch?

DIONYSOS.                        All right.    200

CHARON.  *Surely* you'll put up your arms and stretch
    out?

DIONYSOS.    OK.

CHARON.  Stop acting up! Brace your foot!
Pull hard!

DIONYSOS.    And how do I
who am unpracticed, unshipshape, and unnaval,
row the boat?

CHARON.    Very easily. You'll hear such                    205
beautiful songs once you lay to.

DIONYSOS.                    Whose?

CHARON.  Marvels of the frog-swans.

DIONYSOS.                    Beat the measure!

CHARON.  *One*, two, three; *one*, two, three. ὠὸπ ὄπ ὠὸπ ὄπ

**191.** See note on line 33.

60 *Aristophanes*

(DIONYSOS, *rowing to* CHARON'*s triple beat, is challenged
offstage by a double-beat chorus from the* FROGS.)

CHORUS OF FROGS. (*Ghosts of Frogs*)   ∪∪∪ − ∪ − ∪ −

βρεκεκεκὲξ   Brécka-keck-kéx, co-ácks, co-ácks.   *iambotrochaic
with enoplic &
prosodiac*

210   κοὰξ κοὰξ   Brecka-keck-kex, co-acks, co-acks.

Children of the marshy springs,
Make a flutelike cry that sings,
Following the hymnlike flute,
Sounding our sweet co-acks toot,

215   Our co-acks for Dionysos,
Zeus' Son who dwells at Nysus.
In the marshes there we shout,
When mobs march Athenian groves
In a rambling, drunken rout,
For the potted treasure troves.

220   Brecka-keck-kex, co-acks, co-acks.
DIONYSOS.
I start to feel my bum has cracks,
You croakers of co-acks, co-acks.
FROGS.   Brecka-keck-kex, co-acks, co-acks.
DIONYSOS.
Your only care is for these quacks.
225   FROGS.   Brecka-keck-kex, co-acks, co-acks.
DIONYSOS.
May you drop dead with your co-acks!
You're nothing but your old co-acks.
FROGS.   Doubtless you are right, Butt-inski,
But the lyre-skilled muse commends me,
230   Goat-foot Pan who blows the reeds.
And Apollo more concedes,
Since I nourish his lyre's bridges,
Stalks that grow among my sedges.
235   Brecka-keck-kex, co-acks, co-acks.
DIONYSOS.  I have got blisters, and my bum
Is sweating and it starts to hum.
When it pops out, then it will say—

**216, Nysus.** The name of several places connected to Dionysos and
may derive from the last part of the god's name.

FROGS.    Brecka-keck-kex, co-acks, co-acks!
DIONYSOS.    But, O race of lovers of song,    240
                Desist!
FROGS.                Oh no, we must prolong
                Singing, who in sunny vale
                Ever hopped through galingale
                Or reeds, joying in our croon,
                Often-plunging limbs in tune.    245
                Or when, fleeing the abundance
            Of god's rain, we call our fun-dance,
            Nimble steps, up through an ocean
                With our bubbloblustermotion. πομφολυγοπαφλάσμασεν
DIONYSOS.
                Brecka-keck-kex, co-acks, co-acks:    250
                I shall snatch that call from you.
FROGS.            We will suffer if you do.
DIONYSOS.    I myself am suffering worst,
                If I row, until I burst.    255
FROGS.    Brecka-keck-kex, co-acks, co-acks.
DIONYSOS. Damn you! you are zilch to me.
FROGS.        Righto, we'll play too and see.
            We shall scream and stretch, and splay
            Our throats wide as we can all day—    260
DIONYSOS.
                Brecka-keck-kex, co-acks, co-acks.
                *You* won't conquer *me* that way.
FROGS.        *You* won't conquer *me* at all.
DIONYSOS.  *You* won't send me to the wall,
                Never. I shall scream your call,
                If it means all day I bawl,    265
                Till I rule over your co-acks:
                Brecka-keck-kex, co-acks, co-acks!
    *(silence)*
            I knew I'd break the backs of your co-acks.
CHARON.    Stop, stop! Lay in with the oar!
        Get out. Fork over the fare.

**243, galingale.** A species of sedge.

270   DIONYSOS.                         Two obols!
*(Exit* CHARON *with his boat.)*
Xanthias. Where's Xanthias? O, Xanthias!
*(*XANTHIAS *enters.)*
     XANTHIAS.   Yoo-hoo!  ἰαῦ
     DIONYSOS.               Walk over here.
     XANTHIAS.                              Good day, my lord.
     DIONYSOS.   What is here?
     XANTHIAS.                   Dark and muck.
     DIONYSOS.   Did you see the father-beaters there
and the oath-breakers he told us of?

275   XANTHIAS. *(pointing to the audience)*   Don't you?
     DIONYSOS.   By Poseidon, I see them now.


Come, what do we do?
     XANTHIAS.                  Best to go on,
since this is the place where dreadful
beasts are, as he said—
     DIONYSOS.              He'll regret it.
280 He exaggerated, so I would be scared;
knowing what a warrior I am, he was jealous.
Nothing conquers Heracles' arrogance.
But I pray to encounter something and make
a triumph worthy this journey.

285   XANTHIAS.   By Zeus, but I hear a noise!
     DIONYSOS.   W-w-w-where?  ποῦ ποῦ 'στιν;
     XANTHIAS.                Behind.
     DIONYSOS.                        Get behind!
     XANTHIAS.   But it's in front.
     DIONYSOS.                   Now go in front!
     XANTHIAS. *(pretending)*   By Zeus, I see a frightful
         beast.
     DIONYSOS.   What kind?
     XANTHIAS.                Awful. It becomes everything.
290 Now a bull, now a mule, then some woman,
quite ripe.
     DIONYSOS.   Where? I'm going after her.
     XANTHIAS.   Not a woman now—she's a dog.

*Empousa* [handwritten in top margin]

DIONYSOS. That's Empousa!

XANTHIAS.                              Lit by fire,
her whole face.

*Empusa* [handwritten margin note]

DIONYSOS.      Has she a bronze leg?

XANTHIAS. By Poseidon, yes. And the other one's
   cow dung,                                                        295
you know.

DIONYSOS.   Where can I turn?

XANTHIAS.                              And I?

DIONYSOS. *(to his priest seated in front of the
   audience)* My priest, protect me—and we'll have
   drinks later.

*turns to priest in audience* [handwritten margin note]

XANTHIAS. We're ruined, Lord Heracles!

DIONYSOS.                              Don't call me that!
Dear sir, I beg you, don't say that name.

XANTHIAS. Dionysos, then.

DIONYSOS.                              That's worse than the
                                             other.                      300

XANTHIAS. Thither, demon! Here, here, Master.

DIONYSOS. What?

XANTHIAS.            Take heart. We've done well.
We can say like that actor:
"After the storm, the sea clams—calms!—down."
Empousa is gone.

DIONYSOS.      Swear it!

XANTHIAS.                              By Zeus.                      305

DIONYSOS. Again!

XANTHIAS.            By Zeus.

DIONYSOS.                  Swear!

XANTHIAS.                              By Zeus!

DIONYSOS. Poor me, how I turned white seeing her.

XANTHIAS. *(looking at* DIONYSOS' *rear)* Rather fear
   made you orange.

**293, Empousa.** A popular goblin who could change shape.
**304, "After ... down."** In Euripides' *Orestes* (1. 279), an actor
named Hegelochus somehow mispronounced *galén'* (= *galena*,
"calm things") making it into a "polecat" (*galên*): "After the
storm, I see a polecat."
   *weasel* [handwritten note]

*the polecat after the storm ...* [handwritten margin note]

64 *Aristophanes*

DIONYSOS. Alas, whence have we fallen on such evil?

310 What god shall I charge with my destruction?

XANTHIAS. "Air, Zeus' cottage," or "The foot of
Time"?

*(Someone plays flute music within.)*

There!

DIONYSOS. What is it?

XANTHIAS. Don't you hear?

DIONYSOS. What?

XANTHIAS. A breath of flutes.

DIONYSOS. Yes, and a breeze
of torches breathed on me, so mystical!

315 But quiet; let us crouch and listen in.

CHORUS. *(offstage)*

(TRUE PARODOS?)

Iacchos, Iacchos, Iacchos!

*bacchiac di*
*trimeters*

XANTHIAS. That's them, my Lord, your Initiates,
dancing here, the ones he told us of.

320 Anyway they sing Iacchos, like the atheist.

DIONYSOS. That's right. Now it's best to keep
calm so we'll know for sure.

TRUE PARODOS
Str.

CHORUS.

Iacchós, honóred greatly, dwelling in these precincts,

325 Iacchos, Iacchos, Iacchos!

Enter dancing on this meadow;

*ionios*

To your pious bands,

Tossing your crown,

Teeming with fruit

330 Of myrtle, boldly treading

The untrammeled,

Playful worship,

335 Shared by all the Graces—pure, devout

Dance of mystic choirs.

XANTHIAS. O revered and royal daughter of Demeter,
what sweet pig meat I smell!

**316, Iacchos.** "The Roarer," another name for Dionysos.
**320, the atheist.** Diagoras, a notorious atheist, used to mock the
mysteries with their own cry.

DIONYSOS. Won't you stay still? You may get some
    sausage too.

(CHORUS OF INITIATES *enters.*)

CHORUS.

    Rouse our flaming torches, hands high! You step
        forward,                                *Ant.*

                       340

        Iacchos, Iacchos, Iacchos,
        Star-light bearer to dark rites.
           Meadows glisten fire,
             Ancient knees leap            345
              Casting pain off,
          The cycles of long years,
            Freed by homage.
          Gleaming torchlight,         350
    Lead us forward to the flowery marshland,
       Blest one, lead our youth.

*εὐφημεῖν χρὴ κἀξίστασθαι τοῖς ἡμετέροισι χοροῖσιν* Λ

Back away from our rites, keep a tongue that's devout,
You, the impure, unacquainted with Bacchos' shout.
Neither dancing nor knowing the high muses' meter,
Uninitiated in tonguing the rites of a comic bull-eater;
Who rejoice in crude jokes made at all the wrong
    times
And won't break with hated faction, though sick of
    their crimes.
But you rouse and fan flames for your personal desire.
Or, when Athens is storm-tossed, are ruler for hire:
Selling a fort or a ship, or exporting contraband;
At Aegina, a fiendish collector of duties—underhand—

*[margin annotations: ANAP. tetram. 354-83; ABORTIVE PARABASIS 355 warning to profani; no coarse humor; 360 no demagogues]*

---

**357, a comic bull-eater.** Cratinus, the "comic bull-eater," was
the most celebrated of Aristophanes' predecessors in writing
comedy. He defeated Aristophanes' *The Clouds* in the dramatic
competition of 423 B.C. Worshippers of Dionysos ate the raw
flesh of sacrificed bulls.

**363, At Aegina . . . underhand.** Aegina is an island near Athens.
The collector of duties is Thorycion, probably a corrupt customs
official. He is also the taxman referred to at the end of the short
song below (line 382).

Shipping pitch, oar-bags, and canvas to Epidaurus;
*no traitors*
Or persuading some traitor to outfit the ships that will
365      gore us;
Crapping on Hecate's shrines with melodious lay;
Or, as leader of Athens, you nibble tragedians' pay
Once you are mocked in the comical bacchanal rites.
I proclaim, I proclaim, I proclaim it all thrice:
Be these far from the mystical dance. So now waken
370      your song,
And our vigils all night, in the festivals where they
      belong.

*procession starts*
*TRUE PARODOS*
  *CONT.*
   *str. a*
        All dance, bravely now.     *spondaic*
        In the meadows'
        Sweet womb, tread hard.
        Jeer, play
375        And mock—
        For breakfast was a godsend.

   *ant. a*
        But go, nobly praise
        Now the Goddess;
        Sing loud; she vows
380        To save
        Our land—
        Each season from the taxman.

Come now, and raise another bright song to the fruit-
      bearing queen,
Demeter, honoring the goddess with *her* holy paean.

  *str. b*
        O Queen of holy rite,   *iambics*
385        Demeter, stay and help  *384-447*
        To save your sacred chorus,
        And let me play in safety
        All day, and dance.

**364, Epidaurus.** A port in the Peloponnesus.

And grant me many jokes,                    ant.b
    Serious sayings too,                    390
To play, to mock, to conquer
And wear the victor's garlands,
    Worthy your feast.

Dance on!

And now call here the god who flourishes in beauty;    395
Call him in choral song, our cohort in this dance.

Honored Iacchos, find your sweetest         str.c
    Song and follow here
      Before Demeter,                          400
    And show us how, tireless,
You can complete the lengthy way. (12 mi. to Eleusis)
Escort me, Iacchos, lover of the choral dance.
Ἴακχε φιλοχορευτά, συμπρόπεμπέ με.

For you tore my little sandal,              ant.c
    Penny-pinching, and                       405
My old dress for laughter,
    When you found out cheaper
Measures for us to whirl and play.
Escort me, Iacchos, lover of the choral dance.

Just now glancing round I caught sight      epod.c
    Of a little thing,                        410
    Fair-faced, our playmate,
    Who burst a seam; I saw
     τιτθίον
Her well-made breastling peeping out.
Escort me, Iacchos, lover of the choral dance.
XANTHIAS.    I'm always rather ready
      To follow after her,
I want to dance and play.

**404–08, For you . . . play.** One wore old clothes in mystic pro-
cessions. Here also is a reference to the stinginess of patrons in
providing for the chorus during the war.

415     **DIONYSOS.**         Me too!

*str.d*    **CHORUS.**       Do you wish to mock

*v.n.*             The [blear-eyed] power-hawk? *Archedemus*

    At seven he had baby teeth and no Athenian stock,

        And now he demagogues

420           Among the dead above.

    Up there Archedemus is held to be the best of rogues.

        I hear that Cleisthenes

        Is down upon his knees

    Among the graves and tears his tail and grinds his
        cavities;

425         Bent down, he pounds his breast

        Laments and shakes his chest,

        For Sipenis, the Masturbationist.

*ant.d*         And Callias, they say,

        The son of Horsetolay, *'Ιππόβινος*

430     A lion-skin on his *κύσθου* pussy, to war he's sailed away.

    **DIONYSOS.**     Could you tell us both

        Where Pluto hangs about,

    For we are strangers here, who just got off the boat?

    **CHORUS.**     Do not go far from here,

*Archedemus & Theramenes indict generals of Arginusae*

**416–21, Do you wish . . . rogues.** Archedemus was a demagogue,
who along with Theramenes, indicted the generals after Athens'
victory at Arginusae (see note on line 33), because they did not
retrieve the bodies of the dead. Six were executed. At seven
years of age, the age of second teeth, an Athenian child would
be enrolled in the citizenry. Aristophanes often bewails the foreign corruption of Athens.

**422–27, I hear . . . Masturbationist.** For Cleisthenes, see note on
line 49. Sipenis is a made-up comic name.

**428–30, And Callias . . . sailed away.** The profligate Callias squan-
dered his wealth on women and died poor. Had he used up all
his masculinity? His father's name, *Hipponikos*, is altered to *Hip-
pobinos*, "horse-screwer."

Nor ask again to hear, 435
But know that you've arrived now at his very door.

DIONYSOS.   Again, my boy, the baggage!
XANTHIAS.   But what about this garbage?
It means no more to beds than "Son of Zeus," the old
   Corinthian adage.
CHORUS. Go now, 440

*Demeter/Perseph.*
Along the holy circle, in the goddess' flowery grove,
And play, communing in the festival and favored by
   the gods.
     I sway together with the girls and wives. 445
To where they keep our watches, there I bear her
   torch.

*Aeolic*
    Let us go to rose-abounding
    Meadows, patterned with flowers,
     Sporting our winding path 450
    Full of gorgeous dancing.
    That's where the prospering
    Fates assemble.

    We alone receive sun brightness,
     Torchlight that is divine, 455
      Only Initiates:
    We who kept the ritual
    Respect for strangers and
      private men.

*trimeters* DIONYSOS. Now, how should I strike this door? 460 *SYZYGY: EPIRRHEMA*
How do the natives here knock?
   XANTHIAS.   Don't waste time. Bite the doors,
a taste of Heracles' manner and matter.
   DIONYSOS. Boy, boy!

**439, "Son of Zeus" ... adage.** That is, nothing at all. The Cor-
inthians seem to have constantly boasted that their eponymous
founder, Corinthus, was Zeus' son.

Aeacus

70   Aristophanes

(AEACUS *enters*.)

    AEACUS.  Who is it?

    DIONYSOS.          Heracles the Mighty.

*Aeacus'*
*threats*

465    AEACUS.  You nauseous, amoral, brazen,
blood-polluted, blood-covered, most bloody,
who rustled our dog, Cerberus,
leaping, choking, escaping, stealing
the one I guarded. Now you're in our grip.

470 Such Stygian, black-hearted rocks
guard you, and the Acherontian peak
dropping gore, the scurrying dogs of Cocytus,
and the hundred-headed viper, who will sunder
your entrails, and the Tartarean eel

475 who'll seize your lung, and those dry figs,
the Gorgons, who will tear apart
your kidneys bleeding with your bowels,
for whom I'll shake a lightning leg.

(*Exit* AEACUS.)

*Dion. shits*
*self*

    XANTHIAS.  Hey, what have you done?

    DIONYSOS.        I did my duty. Summon the god.

480    XANTHIAS.  You're absurd. Won't you stand up quick
before some stranger sees you?

    DIONYSOS.            But I'm weak.
Bring a sponge for my heart.

    XANTHIAS.  Here, do it yourself—Where? O golden
        gods,
is that where you wear your heart?

*heart in*
*bowel*

    DIONYSOS.            It was afraid
485 and crept down into my lower bowel.

    XANTHIAS.  You're the most gutless of men and gods.

    DIONYSOS.                       Me?
What coward would ask you for a sponge?
No other man would dare it!

    XANTHIAS.             He'd do *what*?

---

**467–76, Cerberus . . . Gorgons.** For Cerberus, see note on line
**111.** Below: **Styx, Acheron,** and **Cocytus** were the three rivers of
Hades. **Tartarean:** belonging to Hades. The **Gorgons** were hideous, female monsters.

DIONYSOS. He would lie down and smell it, if he
    were a coward.
I stood up and wiped myself besides.            490
    XANTHIAS. By Poseidon, real manliness.
    DIONYSOS.                     By Zeus, yes.
You did not fear the thunder of his words
and his threats?
    XANTHIAS.    No, by Zeus, wouldn't think of it.
    DIONYSOS. Come then, since you love boldness and
        are manly,
You become me, and take this club          495
and lion-skin, if you are not faint-hearted.
In turn, I'll be the baggage boy.
    XANTHIAS. Be quick then, for I must obey.
Now look upon Heraclanthias,
if *I'll* be a coward and have *your* spirit.         500
*(They exchange clothing.)*
    DIONYSOS. No, by Zeus, but a true Melitan,
        deserving
—the whip! Let's go. I'll take up this ticking.
*(Enter* SERVANT *of* PERSEPHONE.*)*
    SERVANT. O beloved Heracles, you are here. Come
       in.
When the goddess learned you were coming, at once
she had bread baked, boiled two or three     505
pots of pea soup and roasted a whole steer,
baked honey cakes, rolls—come in.
    XANTHIAS. Marvelous. Thanks, but—
    SERVANT.                  By Apollo, I won't
watch you go off, since she also
made chicken soup, and candied         510
fruit and mixed the most sweet wine.
Come with me.
    XANTHIAS.    Really nice, but—
    SERVANT.              You remain a fool,

---

**501, Melite.** Melite was a district of Athens that had a shrine to
Heracles.

but I'll not let you off. Also there's a flute girl
inside now, in full bloom, and two or three
dancing girls as well.

515   XANTHIAS.               What, dancers?
    SERVANT. In their prime and fresh plucked.
But go in, because the cook
is just taking the fish out
and your table has been brought in.
    XANTHIAS. Go now, tell first the dancing girls
520   inside that I, their master, am coming.
    (*Exit* SERVANT.)


Here, boy, follow us with the bags.
    DIONYSOS. Wait, you! Surely you don't take seriously
my dressing you as Heracles for a joke?
Don't play the fool anymore, O Xanthias,
525   but load and carry the bedding again.
    XANTHIAS. What's this? Surely you yourself don't
         wish
to take back what *you* gave me?
    DIONYSOS.                No *perhaps*, I'm taking it.
Shed the lion-skin!
    XANTHIAS.        I call witnesses
and trust my case to the gods!
    DIONYSOS.                What gods?
530 To think that you—isn't it an absurd vanity?—
a slave and a mortal, could be Alcmena's son?
    XANTHIAS. OK, sure, take 'em. You'll need
me too someday—god willing.
    (*They exchange clothing again.*)

    CHORUS.        From a man of wits
                Come such clever bits:
535            Having sailed 'round much,
             He rolls when he's in Dutch
                To the ship's safe side;
                Rather than abide,
             Like some heroic stone
             That keeps one shape alone;

But turns toward softer down,     540
    The way of cleverness,
      Theramenes' success.

DIONYSOS.     Wouldn't it be a joke:
    Xanthias, who's my bloke,
      On Milesian sheets
    Will kiss some girl off streets,
    Turn and want the pan?
    While I watch the man,
    I'll grasp my chick-pea pod,     545
    And he'll see me, the sod,
    Then rapping on my nod,
    His tight-clenched fist will rout
      My ivory chorus out.

*(Enter* HOSTESS.*)* πανδοκευτρία

trimeters

HOSTESS. Cookie, Cookie, come! Here is
that pig who visited our inn once
and ate sixteen of our loaves—     550
*(Enter* COOKIE.*)*

COOKIE.               By Zeus,
That's the one!

XANTHIAS.    Trouble for someone.

HOSTESS. And meat stewed for twenty beside,
half an obol each—

XANTHIAS.      Someone will pay now.

HOSTESS. And all that garlic.

DIONYSOS.         Foolish woman,     555
You don't know what you're saying.

HOSTESS.          You didn't expect
I'd know you because you wear that boot.
Really? I haven't mentioned all the smoked fish!

COOKIE. Nor by Zeus, your fresh cheese, poor dear,
that he gobbled along with the baskets.     560

HOSTESS. And when I asked for my money,

542y64:
ANTEPIRRHEMA
550
Hostess thinks
she's got
Heracles

541a, **Theramenes.** Nicknamed the "boot," because he changed
political sides often. Cf. note on lines 416–21.
543a, **Milesian.** The city of Miletos produced a very soft wool.

He looked fiery and roared and roared.

XANTHIAS. That's *his* work. Same style everywhere.

HOSTESS. Then drew his sword and seemed to go
    mad.

COOKIE. Poor woman, by Zeus.

565    HOSTESS.                  We two—*somehow* afraid—
leapt up on the sideboard. And he
rushed off taking the rugs with him.

XANTHIAS. That's him too.

HOSTESS.           We should have done something.
Go, call my protector, Cleon,

570 and my Hyperbolus, if you meet him,
so we may crush this man.

*(Turns to* DIONYSOS.*)*

                    You bloody gullet,
how sweet it'd be to smash with a stone
those grinders you used to swill my stock.

DIONYSOS. I'd toss you in the executioner's pit.

575    COOKIE. With a sickle I'd hack your windpipe,
where you gulp down ox guts.
But I'm going to Cleon, who today will wind
that food back out with a summons.

*(Exit* HOSTESS *and* COOKIE.*)*

DIONYSOS. May I die wretched, if I don't love
    Xanthias!

XANTHIAS. I know, *know* your mind; stop, *stop* your

580    talk.
I wouldn't be Heracles again, couldn't.

DIONYSOS.                  Don't,
Xanthy.

XANTHIAS.   How could I be Alcmena's son,
being a slave *and* a mortal?

DIONYSOS. I know, I know, you're angry and do
    right.

585 Even if you strike me I won't complain.

**569–70, Cleon and Hyperbolus.** Athenian demagogues. For
Cleon, cf. "principal dates in the life of Aristophanes."

The Frogs  75

But if I deprive you in the future,
may I, root and branch, wife, children,
die horribly, along with Archedemus, the blear-eyed!           *again they exchange clothing*
    XANTHIAS. I accept your oath. For that I do it.
*(They exchange clothing again.)*                                          SYZYGY:
ANTODE
*trochaic*    CHORUS.        Now this is your task:
                Take again the mask                                   590
                That you wore before.
             Be strong again once more.
             Once again look fierce.
             Mindful god, rehearse
          The way the god would talk.
            But if it's poppycock,
            Or from a coward stock,                                595
            Back you'll be returned
         To bags, a fate you've earned.
    XANTHIAS.        Fairly you advise,
             Men, but I surmise—
            I, by chance, just now—
           If it turns well somehow,
             He will try to steal                                   600
           Back these things, I feel.
           But I will, for my part,
           Put on a hero's heart
          And look like mustard tart.
           It seems I must be stout:
          I hear the door swing out.
*(Enter AEACUS with two attendants.)*                          SCENE 1
*trimeters*    AEACUS. Quick, tie up that dog-stealer                   605
for punishment! Hurry!                                         *Aeacus wants to arrest Heracles for dog rustling*
    DIONYSOS.        Trouble for someone.
    XANTHIAS. Go to hell and stay back!
    AEACUS.                What? Want to fight?
Dermacallus, Scaboon, and Windbreak.
Come here; fight with him!
    DIONYSOS. Isn't it awful that this robber of others'          610

**588, Archedemus.** Cf. note on lines 416–21.

stuff then strikes out?

AEACUS.                    I'd say, horrible!

DIONYSOS. And abominable and—and—and awful.

XANTHIAS.                                      By Zeus,

If I was ever here, may I be dead,

or if I stole worth a hair.

615 I also make you a most generous offer:

Take my servant there and torture him!

If you find me guilty, lead me to death!

AEACUS. How should I torture him?

XANTHIAS.                          Every way. Ladder-

dangling, hanging, flailing, flaying,

620 racking, pouring vinegar in his nostrils,

piling bricks on him, and all the others, except

beating him with a leek or raw onion.

AEACUS. A fair game. And if I mutilate

your slave, insurance is on hand.

625 XANTHIAS. Not necessary at all. To the torture!

AEACUS. Right here then. He'll speak before your
    face.

Put down your baggage and don't utter

any lie here!

DIONYSOS. I proclaim to all:

Don't torture me; I'm a god—

or blame yourself.

630 AEACUS.          *What* are you saying?

DIONYSOS. I say I'm an immortal, Dionysos, Son of
    Zeus,

and this is my slave.

AEACUS.              Hear that?

XANTHIAS.                        I hear.

He must be whipped all the more.

If he is a god, he won't feel it.

635 DIONYSOS. Well, since you also claim divinity,

won't you receive equal blows with me?

XANTHIAS. A fair game. And you will see which of
    us,

being struck, breaks down or notices—

that one, believe me, is no god.

AEACUS. There is no way you are not a gentleman    640
for you go right for justice. Strip!

XANTHIAS. How will you test us fairly?

AEACUS.                               Easy,
blow by blow.

XANTHIAS.    Good idea.

AEACUS. There!

XANTHIAS.      Watch now; see if I flinch!      *Xanthias*

AEACUS. I already hit you.                   *withstands*

XANTHIAS.          By Zeus, it doesn't seem    *pain*
                  so.                                645

AEACUS. I'll go to this one and hit.

DIONYSOS.                  When?

AEACUS. I did.

DIONYSOS.    Why didn't I even sneeze?

AEACUS. Don't know. I'll try the other again.

XANTHIAS. Won't you hurry? A-a-ah! *ἰατταταῖ*    *!*

AEACUS.                Why the "A-a-ah"?
You don't feel pain?

XANTHIAS.        No, by Zeus,            650
just thought of Heracles' feast at Diomeia.

AEACUS. What a saint! Time to go back here.

DIONYSOS. Aye, aye! *ἰοῦ ἰοῦ*

AEACUS.         What is it?

DIONYSOS.            I see some horsemen.

AEACUS. Why cry?                      *Dion. smells*
                                         *onions "*

DIONYSOS.    I smell their onions.

AEACUS. You noticed nothing then?

DIONYSOS.               Nothing bothers me. 655

AEACUS. Must go back to this one.

XANTHIAS. O-o-oh! *οἴμοι*               *Xanthias*

AEACUS.     What?                     *"has a*

XANTHIAS.        Pull out this thorn!    *thorn "*

AEACUS. What's this? Back here now.

---

**651, Diomeia.** A district of Athens.
**654, onions.** Cavalry received rations of onions.

*Dion. shouts "Apollo"— then pretends to be reciting poetry*

DIONYSOS. Apollo!—"Who holdest Delos, Pytho."

XANTHIAS. He felt pain; didn't you hear?

660 DIONYSOS.                                    Not I,

since I was quoting Hipponax's iambics.

XANTHIAS. You're getting nowhere; bash his sides!

AEACUS. By Zeus, stick out that belly!

DIONYSOS. Poseidon!—

XANTHIAS.                    Someone felt it.

DIONYSOS.                                    "In sea depths,

665 thou rulest an Aegean headland and sea-green"—

AEACUS. By Demeter, I still cannot learn

which of you is a god, but go in.

670 The master himself will know you,

and Persephone; they are gods too.

DIONYSOS. Fine idea. I wish you had thought

of this earlier, before I took my beating.

*(AEACUS, two attendants, DIONYSOS, and XANTHIAS exit.)*

PARABASIS:ODE    CHORUS.

*prosodiac enoplic*

O muse, join in the sacred choruses, enjoy

675                     My song,

Look on great multitudes assembled, where all arts

                    Belong,

Devoted more to honor than is⌊Cleophon,⌋

680 Upon whose foreign lips a Thracian swallow rings

                    Such wrong,

While sitting on a barbarous leaf.

He cries the dying nightingale's lament, though votes     *anap.*

685                     Be strong.

---

**661, Hipponax's iambics.** Satirist of the sixth century.

**665, "In sea depths . . . sea-green."** Perhaps a reference to Sophocles' lost *Laocoon*.

**674-737.** The chorus now recites the *parabasis* in a variety of meters. Cf. "introduction."

*hawk who rejected peace*  **679, Cleophon.** He succeeded Theramenes (cf. note on line 541a) as chief demagogue. Aristophanes attacks his citizenship by suggesting he was a Thracian, not an Athenian. His downfall is predicted in spite of support. He was executed the following year.

*trach. tetram.*
*catal.*

To teach our state and recommend the good,
Our holy chorus thinks is just. First, it's
But right to make equal our citizens,
Kill fears. If one was tripped by Phrynichus,
I say we should let those who slipped before
Present their case, and clear their former crimes.
Second, no one should be deprived the rights
Of our city. Yet slaves who fought in ships
But once, are sudden lords with our Plataeans.
And I would not deny that was well done.
But praise it. This alone you thought out well.
Yet it is reasonable also to
Forgive their one mistake at their request.
Their fathers too fought well, and they are natives.
But set aside your rage, O wisest men.
And let us have them willingly as kin,
Enfranchised citizens who'd fight with us.
If we swell up and glorify ourselves,
Steering our city in this seething storm,
Later, we shall appear to have thought poorly.

PARABASIS:
EPIRRHEMA

*oligarchs*
*punished*
690

*slaves given*
*citizenship*

695

*restore*
*citizenship*

700

705

*prosodiac*
*enoplic*

If I can see the life and way of one who soon
        Will bawl,
Not long that wastrel ape will bug us, Cleigenes
        The Small,

PARABASIS:
ANTODE

*democrat*

**689–704, If one . . . storm.** Aristophanes pleads for an amnesty
for those who supported the oligarchical revolution of the Four
Hundred in 411 B.C. The revolution was defeated later that year.
Demagogues like Cleophon, Theramenes, and Cleigenes were
still persecuting the insurgents six years later. **Phrynichus.** This
Phrynichus was a member of the oligarchical revolution of the
Four Hundred. He is not to be confused with the two poets by
that name.

*amnesty for*
*oligarchic*
*supporters*

**693–94, Yet slaves . . . Plataeans.** The slaves freed after the Battle
of Arginusae (cf. note on line 33) were given the limited rights
of citizenship that Athens had extended to the people of Plataea
after the destruction of their city by the Peloponnesians in 427.
**708–14. Cleigenes.** By trade, Cleigenes was a keeper of the baths
and laundry. Good cleansing clay came from the Greek island
of Cimolus, but the corrupt Cleigenes mixes it with inferior
detergents. Politically, he was a minor demagogue and a sup-
porter of Cleophon (cf. note on line 679).

*slaves made*
*citizens*

80   *Aristophanes*

710   The most corrupt of those who manage public baths,
The lordly-waterers-of-lye with phony soap
And marl
From Cimolus. He goes to war,
Lest he someday be stripped when drunk without his
715   staff
And fall.

—∪‒∪|‒∪‒∪|‒∪‒∪|‒∪‒∪|‒
troch. tetram.
catalectic

PARABASIS:
ANTEPIRRHEMA

Often it seems to us the city treats
The same the beautiful, good citizens,
silver 720   And old coinage with newly minted gold.
old coins   No, we won't use money that's undebased,
versus new   Though it be best of all the coin, it's clear,
silver plate   And it alone is rightly struck, and tested
copper coins   In Greece and barbarous countries everywhere.
725   But we prefer the worthless copper coins,
Struck only yesterday in wretched mints.
Those citizens we know well-born and humble,
Brave men and just and good and beautiful,
Trained in the wrestling schools, in dance and arts,
730   We treat basely and use the carrot-tops,
Foreign coppers, and vile in the worst ways,
The new arrivals whom the city used
Before not even for a random scapegoat.
But now, you fools, shift your direction, once
735   Again use the useful, and praise will crown
Success, and if you trip, on noble trees
You'll hang,* suffering what the wise approve.

(*Enter* XANTHIAS *and* SERVANT OF PLUTO.)

EPISODE 1
Pluto's
palace

SERVANT. By our preserver Zeus, your master   trimeters
is a noble man.

XANTHIAS.   How not,   πίνειν   βινεῖν
740   one who knows only drinking and dinking?

SERVANT. Not to beat you, convicted outright,
a slave who claimed to be his master!

XANTHIAS. *He* would have suffered for it.

**730, carrot-tops.** Foreigners.

* cf. proverb: If you hang yourself, do it from a worthy tree.

SERVANT. That certainly
was a slavish trick, the sort I like.
　XANTHIAS. Excuse me, *like*?
　SERVANT. I am ecstatic 745
when I cuss my master in secret.
　XANTHIAS. And grumbling along, when, after
a good beating, you go off?
　SERVANT. Love it.
　XANTHIAS. And meddling a lot?
　SERVANT. By Zeus, I know nothing else.
　XANTHIAS. Zeus of Kinship! And hearing masters, 750
the things they chatter?
　SERVANT. I'm more than mad about it.
　XANTHIAS. What about blabbing it around?
　SERVANT. Me?
By Zeus, when I do, I'm "maniac-ed"!
　XANTHIAS. By Apollo, put your hand there!
Let us kiss together—
*(Shouts are heard offstage.)*

　　　　　　　　　Tell me, 755
By Zeus, who is our fellow-rogue,
what's that uproar and shout
in there and railing?
　SERVANT. Aeschylus and Euripides.
　XANTHIAS. Ah!
　SERVANT. Big, big case under way,
among the dead, and great faction. 760
　XANTHIAS. About what?
　SERVANT. There is a law here
about all the crafts and arts
that the best of all his fellows
gets free meals at City Hall
and a chair next to Pluto.
　XANTHIAS. I see. 765
　SERVANT. Until another arrives, wiser
in his art, then he must yield.
　XANTHIAS. Why does this bother Aeschylus?

best in
professions
dine with
Pluto

SERVANT.  He held the tragic seat, 'cause
he was the greatest in his art.

770   XANTHIAS.                    Who does now?

*Euripides has replaced Aeschylus*

SERVANT.  When Euripides came down, he showed off
to the clothes-grabbers, to the purse-snatchers,
the father-killers, the house-breakers—
hordes of them in Hades. They listened

775   to his counter-arguments, his twists and turns,
went stark mad and thought him wisest,
and then, egged on, he claimed the seat
where Aeschylus sat.

XANTHIAS.              Wasn't he bombarded?

SERVANT.  By Zeus, no, the people called for a trial

780   who was the most skilled in the art.

XANTHIAS.  That assembly of rats?

SERVANT.                    By Zeus, cried to high heaven.

XANTHIAS.  Weren't there others, Aeschylus' allies?

SERVANT.  The good are few, just like there.

*(points to the audience)*

XANTHIAS.  What is Pluto going to do?

*Pluto will call contest & trial*

785   SERVANT.  Call a contest at once, a trial,
a test for both artists.

*ἀγῶνα ποιεῖν...
καὶ κρίσιν*

XANTHIAS.              How come
Sophocles didn't seize the seat?

SERVANT.  Not him, by Zeus. He kissed Aeschylus
when he came down and took his hand.

790   So, he held off from the chair.
Just now he was about to, as Cleidemides said,
sit in reserve. If Aeschylus conquers,

*Soph. will fight Eurip. if he wins*

he keeps his place. If not, he vows
to fight Euripides to the end for his art.

XANTHIAS.  It will happen then?

795   SERVANT.                    By Zeus, not long.
Right here the wonder gets under way.

**791, Cleidemides.** Nothing is known about this man who must
have said he would be an observer and a ready substitute on
some well-known occasion.

Poetry will even be weighed in scales—

poetry will
be weighed

XANTHIAS. What? They'll treat tragedy like lamb?

SERVANT. They'll also bring out rulers and word-
yardsticks and folding frames—

XANTHIAS.                     To make bricks?  800

SERVANT. And miters and wedges, for Euripides says
he shall test tragedy word by word.

XANTHIAS. I think Aeschylus would take that hard.

SERVANT. He did look bullish and crouched down.

XANTHIAS. Who will judge the thing?

SERVANT.                     That's it.  805

Both found a complete shortage of wise men,
and Aeschylus doesn't get on with Athenians—

XANTHIAS. He probably thinks they're a lot of
    housebreakers.

SERVANT. And the rest he believes to be rubbish
as judges of poets, so they have turned  810
to your master, since he's familiar with the art.
But let's go in. Because when our masters
get hot, it's tears for us.

(*Exit* XANTHIAS *and* SERVANT.)

CHORUS.

δεινόν

O now the loud roarer shall swell with awful anger.  STASIMON I

dactylic    When he espies that rival, sharpening his tooth,  815
        That glib-tongued man, his enraged eyes—

troch.              Shall twirl!

Great-crested words and quarrels of the glancing helm,
    Splintering axles of wit, when the fine-carving one
        Fends off the words of the mind-builder's—  820
            High horse.

**814ff.** Much of the remainder of the play is the *agon*, the struggle
(see "introduction") between Aeschylus and Euripides. Aeschylus will mock what he considers low language and corrupt free-
thought in Euripides' plays. Euripides will counter with charges
of wordiness, obscurity, and bombast in the plays of Aeschylus.
The chorus will characterize Aeschylus as a wielder of heroic
phrases ("the loud roarer," line 814) and Euripides as a clever
intellectual ("the fine-carving one," line 819).

84   *Aristophanes*

> Bristling the mane of shaggy hair upon his neck,
> Narrowing awful brows, he'll bellow out word trains,
> Bolted-fast, like ship-planks torn off by his—
> 825                     Grand mouth.

> And then that word-worker and analyst of phrases,
> His smooth tongue shall unroll and jingle envy's bridle,
> Dissect the other's words and split his lungs'—
>                     Big job.

*(Enter* DIONYSOS, *no longer disguised, and* EURIPIDES.)   trimeters

830   EURIPIDES. I won't give up the throne—stop!   θρόνου
I say my art is greater than his.
    DIONYSOS. Aeschylus, why silent? Do you hear this?
    EURIPIDES. First, he'll plump up his glory,
⌊the way he rigs wonders in his tragedies.⌋
835   DIONYSOS. My good man, don't speak too grandly!
    EURIPIDES. I know him and found him long ago
a barbarian poet, an audacious mouth,
unbridled, uncommanded, and unlidded,
unconversational, bombast-bundled—   κομποφακελορρήμονα

*(Enter* AESCHYLUS.)
840   AESCHYLUS. Really you child of a market goddess?
This of me, O Gossipmongerovich,   στωμυλιοσυλλεκτάδη
Street-bum poet, Ragstitcherovich?   ῥακιοσυρραπτάδη
You'll regret your words.
    DIONYSOS.                     Enough, Aeschylus.
Don't heat your heart with angry rancor.
845   AESCHYLUS. Not before I reveal him openly
the poet of the lame, a bold mouth.
    DIONYSOS. A lamb, bring out a black lamb, boys;
a typhoon is about to break out.
    AESCHYLUS. You collected Cretan arias and vile
850   marriages and put them in your work—

**847, a black lamb.** Dionysos calls for a lamb to sacrifice in order
to appease a storm divinity.
**849–50, Cretan arias and vile/marriages.** Cretan songs were in-
novative and nontraditional. "Vile marriages" is used to suggest
relationships like the incestuous love in Euripides' *Hyppolytus.*

DIONYSOS. Hold there, much-honored Aeschylus.
My poor Euripides, clear out
from the hail storm, if you are sane,
lest he whack your skull with a wordy header
from anger and pour out your Telephus. 855
And you, Aeschylus, refute and be refuted
gently. It is not right that poets
abuse each other like bakery women.
You roar like dry oak afire.

EURIPIDES. I'm prepared and I won't hesitate to bite 860
—be bitten first, if he wants—
for my tragic words, songs, and stories,
even for my Peleus and my Aeolus,
my Meleager and especially *my* Telephus.

DIONYSOS. What do you want? Tell me, Aeschylus! 865

AESCHYLUS. I do not wish to struggle down here:
our fight is not equal.

DIONYSOS.                Why not?

AESCHYLUS. Because my works didn't die with me, ❋
but his did, so he can recite them.
But since you think so, I must. 870

DIONYSOS. Someone go, bring frankincense and fire,
so I may pray, before their tricks begin,
to judge this struggle most musically.
*(to the* CHORUS*)*
Some melody for the Muses' rite.

CHORUS.

dactylic          Muses, Virgins of Zeus, you holy nine, 875    ODE
          Who look down on the quibbling wits of men,
              The keen coiners of phrases, who align
              In battle with their studied wrestling zen.
              Please come as well to look on as divine

**855, Telephus.** A king of Mysia, who aided the Greeks in the
Trojan War, and who was the subject and the name of a play
by Euripides, now lost. He once entered the Greek camp disguised as a beggar.
**863–34, Peleus . . . Aeolus . . . Meleager . . . Telephus.** All heroes
from Euripides' plays.

❋ only poet whose works were decreed able to be produced
posthumously!

880   The power of these two most-skilled mouths to pen
      Some phrase and saw to dust some words. Today,
      The contest of the wise is under way.*

885   DIONYSOS. Now pray, you two, before you speak.   trimeters

AESCHYLUS. Demeter, you who nursed my soul,
make me worthy of your mysteries!

   DIONYSOS *(to* EURIPIDES*)* Take incense and put
   it on the fire!

EURIPIDES.          No thanks.

*I* pray to other gods.

DIONYSOS. Some of your own? A new mintage?

890   EURIPIDES.                          Yes, indeed.

DIONYSOS. Go and offer to your strange gods!

EURIPIDES. O *Air*, my fodder! O my pivoting *Tongue*!

My *Native Wit*! My keen-scented *Nostrils*!

Let me rightly confute the words I grasp.

895   CHORUS.          We long to hear      anap. strock.

      From two skilled men what warlike path
         Of words you'll steer.
      The tongue is full of wrath.
      The courage knows no fear.
         The minds are fit.

900      It's likely we are near
         Some clever city bit,
      That's filed down and clear.
   This one will tear the other's wit
   Up, root and branch, and fall on that.
   And scatter far his verbal wrestling mat.   iambic
                                              tetram.

CHORUS LEADER.

905      You must speak very fast and in this way:

Just what is smart, no similes, or what another man
   would say.

EURIPIDES. Very good. What I myself am and my
   poetry is,

I'll show at the close, but first I'll prove this man

A pretentious fake and a cheat, how he swindles

* νῦν γὰρ ἀγὼν σοφίας ὁ μέγας
  χωρεῖ πρὸς ἔργον ἤδη.

The audience, the dullards bred on Phrynichus'
    tragedies.          910
First of all, he would wrap someone up and put him
    in,
Some Achilles, or Niobe, not showing the face—
Just the veneer of tragedy—they didn't even grunt
    like—
*(grunts)*

    DIONYSOS. By Zeus, they didn't.
    EURIPIDES.              And his chorus would
    bang out chains of songs,
Linked four in a row, nonstop, while the rest stayed
    silent.      915

*Eur. on Aesh.'s choruses*

    DIONYSOS. But I enjoyed the silence. It delighted me
No less than those talking nowadays.
    EURIPIDES.            You were silly.
Know it well.
    DIONYSOS. Seems so. Why did our friend do these
              things?
    EURIPIDES. Out of pretentiousness, so the spectator
    would sit speculating
That Niobe would say something, but the play would    920
    go along, along.
    DIONYSOS. The rotten bastard! How I was cheated by
    him!
*(to* AESCHYLUS*)*
Why are you churning and stewing?
    EURIPIDES.          Because I'm finding him out.
And then, when he had acted stupid like this and the
    play
Was half-done, he spoke a dozen ox-heavy words
That have deep brows and crests, and some witch-
    faced horrors,    925
Unknown to the audience.

**910, Phrynichus.** This Phrynichus was a tragic poet and predecessor of Aeschylus.
**912, Achilles, or Niobe.** Achilles was silent in *The Phrygians*, and Niobe was silent in *Niobe*, both lost plays by Aeschylus.

AESCHYLUS.                    Good grief!

DIONYSOS.                              Keep quiet.

EURIPIDES.  He wouldn't utter clearly one—

DIONYSOS *(to* AESCHYLUS*)*          Don't saw your teeth!

*Aeschts's*
*bombast*

EURIPIDES.  But either Scamander rivers or trenches
    or bronze-forged
Griffin-eagles on shields, or huge, horse-cliffed words,
Which were never, ever clear.

930        DIONYSOS.                    By the gods, that's right,
Then I would lie awake in the dead of night
Wondering what kind of bird a golden horsecock is.

AESCHYLUS.  The emblem blazed on ships, you grand
    ignoramus!

DIONYSOS.  I thought it was Eryxis, Philoxenus' Son,
    the cock-fighter.

EURIPIDES.  Why did he have to put even a cock in
935    tragedy?

DIONYSOS.  But you, O Enemy of the Gods, what did
    *you* create?

*Eurip.*
*slimmed*
*down*
*tragedy*

EURIPIDES.  No horsecocks, by Zeus, nor goat stags,
Like you, the ones they draw on Persian tapestries.
When I first took the tragic art from you
940 She was bloated with boasts and weighty words.
Straightaway I drained her and removed her heaviness
With versicles and walking and white beet root,
Giving her doses of babble filtered from books
And nourished her on solo songs—

DIONYSOS.                    Stirring in your
                wife's lover,  *slave of Eurip.*
*Cephisodon*                Cephisophon?

EURIPIDES.  Whatever I did, I did nothing stupid, nor
945    fell into confusion

**932, golden horsecock.** The golden hippolector, a horse with the
wings and tail of a cock, was mentioned by Aeschylus in his lost
*Myrmidons.*

**934, Eryxis, Philoxenus' Son.** Philoxenus was a notorious glutton.
Nothing is know of Eryxis.

**944, Cephisophon.** Lived in the same house with Euripides and
was said to be his wife's lover. —— *and collaborator!*

But right away, at the play's beginning, someone
    would come
And give its genealogy—

DIONYSOS.          Better than your own, by Zeus!

EURIPIDES. Then from the first speech I left no one
    idle.

*everyone spoke in Eurip.'s plays*

But my woman spoke nothing less than my slave
And the ruler, the virgin, and the old woman.

AESCHYLUS.                 Yes, indeed 950
Shouldn't you have died for these outrages?

EURIPIDES.             No, by Apollo,
For I acted democratically.

DIONYSOS.     Let that go, old boy,
That's not the best route for *you* to take.

EURIPIDES. *(pointing to the audience)* Why, I taught
    these people to talk.

AESCHYLUS. *(perhaps covering his ears)*     I'll say!
Would that your tummy had burst open before that! 955

EURIPIDES. And I introduced fine word-squares and
    rulers;

*Eurip. taught subtlety*

To think, see, understand, love twisting and art,
To suspect, be over-subtle in all things.

AESCHYLUS.                I'll say!

EURIPIDES. Brought in domestic matter, helpful to us,
    engaging,

*wrote about the familiar*

In which I could be confuted. For those who knew 960
Would have condemned my art. But I didn't play the
    braggadochio,
Tearing down thought, nor shocked them,
Making Cycnuses and Memnons with jingle-bell horse
    armor.

**963–67, Making Cycnuses . . . are mine.** Cycnus and Memnon
were Trojan allies slain by Achilles. Cycnus appeared in one of
Aeschylus' plays, but we do not know which one. Memnon appeared in two lost plays by Aeschylus, the *Memnon* and *Psychotasia*. Phormisius, whose name suggests "shaggy," was a noted
politician. Cleitophon was an associate of Socrates. Megaenetus is
unknown. For Theramenes, see notes on lines 541a and 689–704.

You will recognize our disciples, his and mine:

That man's shaggy Phormisius and Megaenetus, the
965      Dimwit,

Trumpet-blowing spear-beards and mocking flesh-ripper
pine-benders,

While Cleitophon and Theramenes, the Smart, are
mine.

    DIONYSOS.  Theramenes? Wise and dreadful in all
ways.

Who, if he falls in with mischief, plays close,

Then drops out. A gambler not from Chios, but from
970      Chaos.

    EURIPIDES.  I myself have taught
Them to think such things,
By making artful thought,
And shrewd examinings.
975      So they'll know all the more
Household economy,
Better than before.
And look perceptively,
Then ask, "What is amiss?"
"Where's that?" and "Who took this?"

980    DIONYSOS.  By the gods, these days,
Every one goes in
And screams before his slaves
To ask, "Where is the pot?
Who ate the fish's fin?
985      What about the cup
That last year died on me?
Where's that new garlic knot?
Who sliced this olive up?"
Before they sat on stools,
Brimmed with stupidity,
990      Momma's boys who'd grin,
The sons of fools.

---

**970, Chios.** A Greek island.

*[handwritten marginalia:]* AGON: PNIGOS — Eurip. taught audience to think, to question, to use logic

*[handwritten marginalia, right:]* melodramatic iambic hypermeter — ⏑⏑ ∪ – ⏑⏑ ∪ –

*Aeschylus responds* (handwritten)

CHORUS. (*to* AESCHYLUS)

    This you perceive,
  Shining Achilles; what shall you say?
     Just don't take leave
    Of mind and race astray      995
    From dread recitative.
     But come, O Knight,
   With anger don't conceive.
   Reef in your sails' flight;
  All but the tips retrieve.      1000
   Then more and more incite
  Your ship; take care you watch for when
 You get a smooth breeze settling in again.

CHORUS LEADER.

*anapaestic tetrameters* (handwritten)

Builder of towers of holiest words, first of all Greeks
Who trick out of tragic trumpery, sluice open now
   your creeks.

AESCHYLUS. I am enraged at my misfortune; my heart
  is vexed
If I must answer him. But lest he say I can't—
Tell me, what makes a poet wondered at? *τίνος οὕνεκα* (handwritten)

EURIPIDES. Advice and cleverness and because we
  make *δεξιότητος καὶ νουθεσίας, ὅτι βελτίους τε ποιοῦμεν*
  *τοὺς ἀνθρώπους ἐν ταῖς πόλεσιν* (handwritten)
The citizens better.

*what makes poet wondered at?* (handwritten)

AESCHYLUS.     If you did not,     1010
But made them base who were once good and true,
What fate would you proclaim?

DIONYSOS.     Why death. Don't ask.

AESCHYLUS. Now, see what men he got from me,
Nobly born and tall, not dodging duty,
Not loafers or low life—like now—nor rogues,     1015
But those who breathe lance spear and snow-crowned
  helm,
Casque, greaves, and ox-hide passions seven-fold.

*Aesch's noble characters* (handwritten)

EURIPIDES. His crimes take wing.

DIONYSOS.     His helmet-hammering is killing me.

EURIPIDES. And how did you ennoble these men?

DIONYSOS. Aeschylus, speak; don't be so stiffly proud
  in anger.  *αὐθαδῶς . . . χαλεπῶς* (handwritten)     1020

*tragedy &*
*war*

AESCHYLUS. By making a tragedy brim with Mars.

DIONYSOS.                                        What's that?

*Seven was*
*Inspirational*

AESCHYLUS.                          *Seven Against Thebes.*
Every man who saw it desired to be warlike.

DIONYSOS. This was badly done, since you made the
      Thebans

*made*
*Thebans*
*fiercer !*

Fiercer in the war. For this alone you should be
      whipped.

AESCHYLUS. *You* could have trained too, but were not
1025      inclined.

*Persians*

Then later I produced my *Persians* and taught
The desire to conquer, marshalling the noblest act.

DIONYSOS. *(looking off into space)*
I really loved it when you, O child of dead Darius,
      shrieked,
And suddenly the chorus clapped and said, "Alas!"

AESCHYLUS. Poets must do these things. See how
1030      helpful
To us the noble poets have been: Orpheus brought
His rites and kept us from murder. Musaeus, complete
      cure
Of disease and oracles. And Hesiod, works of the
      earth,
Season of the crops and plowing, and from what
Did godlike Homer have honor and fame, except he
1035      taught good things:
Battle lines, valor, and arming of men?

DIONYSOS.                          He didn't teach Pantacles,
That's for sure, the clumsy clod. The other day as
      escort,
He tied his helmet on; then tried to attach the crest!

AESCHYLUS. And many others, including even the
      hero, Lamachus.

---

**1028–29, O child of dead Darius . . . "Alas."** The "Child of Dead
Darius" is Xerxes, leader of the Persians. The chorus shouts
something similar to "Alas!" in Aeschylus' *Persians* (117, 122,
1070–01) where Xerxes is a character.
**1036, Pantacles.** Unknown.
**1039, Lamachus.** A great Athenian general. — *Sicilian Expedition*

My mind, molded by Homer, created much greatness,

Patrocluses, Teucers, lion-hearts, so I might rouse the citizen

To strain after these when he hears the trumpet.

But, by Zeus, I made no whoring Phaedras nor Stheneboeas,

Nor did anyone see a lady in love in my plays.

  EURIPIDES. By Zeus, no Aphrodite in you!

  AESCHYLUS.              Not in me,

But *on you* and yours she sat full hard,

So much that she threw you down.

  DIONYSOS.         By Zeus, she did that.

What you made other wives do, struck you down yourself.

  EURIPIDES. And what damage, your wickedness, did my Stheneboeas do the city?

  AESCHYLUS. You convinced noble women and the wives of noble men

To drink hemlock, ashamed because of your Bellerophons.

  EURIPIDES. Was the story I composed about Phaedra untrue?

  AESCHYLUS. By Zeus, no, but the poet should conceal wickedness,

Not bring it in or teach it. For the little ones

Have a teacher to show the way, but young men have the poets.

⌞So we must speak good things.⌟ πάνυ δὴ δεῖ χρηστὰ λέγειν ἡμᾶς

---

**1041, Patrocluses, Teucers.** Patroclus and Teucer are heroes in Homer's *Iliad*.

**1043, Phaedras nor Stheneboeas.** Phaedra's incestuous love for her stepson occurs in Euripides' *Hippolytus*. Stheneboea's adulterous love for Bellerophon was the subject of a lost Euripidean play with her name as title. Rejected by Bellerophon, Stheneboea committed suicide.

**1047, So much ... down.** Cf. note on line 944.

EURIPIDES. If you puffed up the grandeurs
Of Mount Lycabettuses and Parnassuses, it was to
teach the good?
We should speak like men.

AESCHYLUS. You perversity, great opinions
And ideas must bear phrases equally great.
1060 It is right that demigods use grander phrases
And that they wear clothing much more majestic than
ours.
What I introduced properly, you corrupted.

EURIPIDES. Doing
what?

*Eurip. put kings in rags*

AESCHYLUS. First, you covered those playing kings
with rags,
So they would appear pitiable.

EURIPIDES. What harm did that do?

AESCHYLUS. For one thing no rich man will outfit a
1065 warship.
But he wraps himself in rags, wails, and cries poor.

DIONYSOS. By Demeter, he has a gown of fleecy
wool underneath.
If this trick works, he pops off to the fish emporium.

AESCHYLUS. And you taught men to pursue the chit-
chat and garble
That emptied the wrestling schools and to massage the
1070 rumps
Of babbling boys and persuaded the flagship men
To rebut their commanders. Yet, when I was alive,
They knew only to call for hard bread and say,
"Yoho!" *ῥυππαπαῖ — rhythmical cry by which oars kept in unison*

DIONYSOS. By Apollo, and fart in the mouth of the
lower rower *προσπαρδεῖν*
1075 And dung his messmate and go off and mug someone.
Now he talks back and no longer rows: just sails here
and there.

**1057, Mount Lycabettuses and Parnassuses.** Mt. Lycabettus is in
Athens. Mt. Parnassus is near Delphi.
**1068, fish emporium.** Fish was an expensive delicacy.

anapaestic AESCHYLUS.

—-ǀᴗᴗ-ǀ-ǀᴗᴗ-

AGON:
ANTEPIRRHEMA
ANTIPNIGOS

What crime is he not guilty of?
Did not this man instruct the panders
And those who bear their babes in temples, 1080
And those who mingle with their brothers,
And those who say that life is death?
From these our city has filled up
With undersecretariats,
And democratic ape buffoons 1085
Who dupe the population daily.
From lack of training now, no one
    Can run the sacred torch.

DIONYSOS.

By Zeus, they can't. So I dried up
With laughter at the festival 1090
When a slow man ran with head down,
Palefaced and fat, falling behind,
A frightful job. Cerameicans
Who waited at the gates struck at
His belly, sides and flanks, and rump, 1095
Till beaten by their flattened hands,
He broke a little fluff upon
    His fading torch and fled.

CHORUS.

AGON:
METAGONIC ODE

trochaic

A great action we have in store, much strife, and
violent war.
    A tough task to decide: 1100
    When one presses the more,
The other one can turn and ride and with sharp force
defend his side.
    But do not just sit still,
For many and varied are wit's attacks.
    The power you have to kill, 1105
    Speak out, charge in, take up
    The old and the new facts.
Venture to drink from subtle wisdom's cup.

**1093, Cerameicans.** Cf. note on line 129.

96 *Aristophanes*

Don't let this strike you dead with fear: no ignorance
dwells here

1110                 Among these spectators
              Whom your sharp wit will cheer.
Don't fear to launch your metaphors: no longer are
they boors,
                For they served in the field
           And have a book and comprehend your wit.
1115                 These natures never yield,
              But now they have been honed.
                So do not fear a bit,
          But marshal all, their skill in art's well known.

EURIPIDES. Now I shall turn to your prologues   *trimeters*
      themselves,
1120 so I may test the first part,
the very beginning of your cleverness.
    DIONYSOS. To which will you apply the touchstone?
    EURIPIDES.                       To quite a few.
First recite the opening of your *Orestes* story.
1125     DIONYSOS. Everyone quiet now! Speak, Aeschylus!
    AESCHYLUS.
        "Conductor of the Dead, Hermes, who holds
        Paternal power, a savior be to me.
        I come back to this land, and I return!"
    DIONYSOS. What's to censure here?
    EURIPIDES.               More than twelve things.
1130     DIONYSOS. But it's all no more than three lines!
    EURIPIDES. Each line has twenty errors.
    DIONYSOS. *(to* AESCHYLUS *who moves to object)*
Aeschylus, I recommend silence. If not,
you may owe more than three lines.
    AESCHYLUS. Am I to keep silent?
    DIONYSOS.                    If you'll listen to
                        me.

**1126–28, "Conductor . . . return!"** The opening lines of Aeschylus' *Choephoroi* ("Libation Bearers"), the Orestes section of his *Oresteia*. — missing in Aesch. MSS!

EURIPIDES. Straightoff he made a sky-high error.          1135

AESCHYLUS. You know you're ridiculous.

EURIPIDES.                    Matters little to me.

AESCHYLUS. Why do you claim I'm wrong?

EURIPIDES.                    Speak again the opening.

AESCHYLUS.

"Conductor of the Dead, Hermes, who holds
Paternal power."

EURIPIDES.          Doesn't Orestes speak this
on his dead father's grave?

AESCHYLUS.              Nothing less.          1140

EURIPIDES. Since his father, Agamemnon, was
butchered
by his mother's hand in a treacherous plot,
is that why he says Hermes keeps paternal powers?

AESCHYLUS. Not at all. He called the Luck-Bringer
Hermes, Conductor of the Dead, saying          1145
clearly that he has this gift from Father Zeus.

EURIPIDES. Your error was worse than I thought.
if he has his father's gift of the dead—

DIONYSOS. Then he would be a graverobber from his
father.

AESCHYLUS. Dionysos, you're drinking a bad bouquet,  1150

DIONYSOS. Give him another one, and *you* find the
flaw.

AESCHYLUS.      "A savior be to me.
I come back to this land, and I return."

EURIPIDES. Twice wise Aeschylus said the same thing.

DIONYSOS. How twice?

EURIPIDES.              Note the phrase; I'll say it:  1155
"I come back to this land," he says, "and I return."
"I come back" is the same as "I return."

DIONYSOS. By Zeus, just as one might say to a
neighbor:
"Lend me a dough-board, or, if you please, a board
for dough."

AESCHYLUS. Not at all, chatter-man,          1160
that contains the best of phrasing.

EURIPIDES. How? Teach me how so.

AESCHYLUS. One who has a homeland "comes back."
He has come without other complication.
A man in flight "comes back" and "returns" from
1165    exile.

DIONYSOS. Good, by Apollo! What say, Euripides?

EURIPIDES. I say Orestes didn't "*return*" home,
but secretly "came back," not asking the authorities.

DIONYSOS. Well done, by Hermes!

                          (aside) I don't get it though.

EURIPIDES. Continue on.

1170 DIONYSOS.                Come, say it,
Aeschylus, hurry, and *you* spot the fault.

AESCHYLUS.

    "Upon this mound of tomb, I call my father
    To give ear and to listen."

*more repetition redundancy*

EURIPIDES.               He says it again.
"Give ear" and "listen" are blatantly the same.

1175 DIONYSOS. But he speaks to the dead, you rotter.
Speaking even triplets we don't reach them.

AESCHYLUS. And how did *you* make your prologues?

EURIPIDES.                      I'll tell you.
If I say the same twice, or you see stuffing
beyond the sense, spit on me!

1180 DIONYSOS. Come, speak. I just must hear
the rightness of your prologues.

*Eurip. recites Oed.*

EURIPIDES. "A well-blest man was Oedipus at first."

AESCHYLUS. No, by Zeus, but cursed in nature,
who, before he was born, Apollo said
1185 would kill his father—before he even was!—
how could he be "well-blest at first"?

EURIPIDES.

    "Then he became the wretchedest of men."

*Aesch's précis of Oed. tyr.*

AESCHYLUS. By Zeus, not at all! He never stopped.
How could he? Exposed as soon as born


**1182, "A well-blest man . . . at first."** From Euripides' lost *Antigone*.

in winter, in a broken pot                                            1190
so he wouldn't be reared his father's killer,
then he limped on bad feet to Polybus,
and after, though young, married the old woman
who was also his own mother.
Then blinded himself.

DIONYSOS.                    Then he was "well-blest"        1195
if he was condemned with General Erasinides. *

EURIPIDES. You're daft. I make fine prefaces.

AESCHYLUS. By Zeus, I'll not nip at each phrase
word by word but with the gods' help
I'll wreck your prologues with an oil flask.                  1200

EURIPIDES. My prologues with an oil flask?

AESCHYLUS.                              Just one.
You write so that anything fits
in your lines—"fleecie," "flaskie,"
"baggie." I will show you straight off.

EURIPIDES. Really, you?

AESCHYLUS.              Yep.

DIONYSOS.                    You must recite.               1205

EURIPIDES.
   "Aegyptus, as the farflung tale has spread,
    By oar of ship with his own fifty sons
    Held Argos fast"—                   *ληκύθιον*

AESCHYLUS.                  "And lost his oil flask."        *oil flask*

EURIPIDES. Why this oil flask? Let it perish!

DIONYSOS. Speak another, so I'll know more.                 1210

EURIPIDES.
   "O Dionysos, wielder of the thyrsos,
    In torch and fawnskin on Parnassus height,

---

**1192, Polybus.** The king of Corinth who adopted Oedipus.
**1196, Erasinides.** One of the generals executed after the Battle
of Arginusae. Cf. note on lines 416–21.
**1200, oil flask.** Athenians carried a vial of skin lotion with them.
Aeschylus uses it to attack what he considers the monotony of
Euripides' verse and his use of trivial details.
**1206–08, "Aegyptus ... fast."** Beginning of Euripides' lost *Archelaus?*

*A blind general could not have been victorious at Arginusae and
thus would have been spared afterward.*

          Who leapt dancing"—

AESCHYLUS.               "And lost his oil flask."

DIONYSOS. Alas, again, we're struck by the flask!

1215  EURIPIDES. That doesn't matter. In *this*

prologue he can't stick in his oil flask:


      "There is no man who's blest in everything:

      Either born-great he has no livelihood,

      Or is ill-born"—

AESCHYLUS.           "And lost his oil flask."

DIONYSOS. Euripides!

EURIPIDES.        What?

DIONYSOS.               Better drop sail.

1220  This oil flask will blow a storm.

    EURIPIDES. By Demeter, I care not.

Now *this* one will knock it from him.

    DIONYSOS. Come, speak another, and avoid the flask.

    EURIPIDES.

1225           "Sidonian Cadmus left his city once,

            Agenor's child"—

AESCHYLUS.                "And lost his oil flask."

DIONYSOS. My good man, buy off the flask,

Or he'll scrape away our prologues.

    EURIPIDES.                 What?

*I* buy him off?

    DIONYSOS.    If you'll listen to me.

    EURIPIDES. Never, since I can recite many prologues

1230  where he can't attach his flask:


      "Tantalian Pelops came to Pisa's land

      On flying mares"

AESCHYLUS.               "And lost his oil flask."


**1211–13, "Dionysos . . . dancing."** From the lost *Hypsipyle*. The
thyrsos was the long wand carried by the bacchants, followers
of Dionysos. Also they wore fawnskins.

**1217–19, "There is . . . ill-born."** From the lost *Stheneboea*.

**1225–26, "Sidonian . . . child."** From the lost *Phrixus*.

**1232–33, "Tantalian . . . mares."** From *Iphigeneia in Tauris*.

DIONYSOS. See? Again he attached his flask.
Good sir, fork over now all you can:  1235
You'll have it for an obol, a fine good one too.
  EURIPIDES. Not yet, by Zeus! I've many left:

  "Oeneus reaped"—
AESCHYLUS.          "And lost his oil flask."
EURIPIDES. Let me recite the whole verse:

  "Oeneus reaped from earth abundant corn,  1240
    Offered first fruits"—
AESCHYLUS.          "And lost his oil flask."
DIONYSOS. While sacrificing? But who stole it?
EURIPIDES. Let it pass, my friend. Let him speak to
    this:

  "Lord Zeus, as it was said by Truth itself"—
DIONYSOS. You'll kill me! He'll say, "And lost his oil
    flask."  1245
This flask goes in all your prologues,
as warts grow on your eyelids.
By the gods, turn now to his lyric songs.
  EURIPIDES. Indeed, I have evidence there what a
    poor,
monotonous melodist he always was.  1250
  CHORUS.    What then shall here resound?
            For I anticipate
            That faults will now be found
            In him who's truly great
            At making lyric sound  1255
            'Mongst those who lived of late.

            I wonder how
            He'll censure now
            The tragic laird.
            For him I'm scared.  1260

1238, "Oeneus reaped." From the lost *Meleager*.
1244, "Lord Zeus . . . itself." From *Melanippe the Wise*.

*[margin: EPISODE 2 CONT.]*

EURIPIDES. True wonders, as shall soon be clear.
I'll whittle all to his one pattern.

DIONYSOS. Taking some pebbles, I'll keep score.
*(Someone plays a flute song.)*

*[margin: (flute music)]*

EURIPIDES. *(with burlesque exaggeration)*   *[margin: mock dactyls]*
"O Phthian Achilles you hear the man-slaying—
*[margin: ἰή, κόπον]* Alas!—stroke! Why the rescue are you now
1265       delaying?"

"To Hermes, first-born of our race, we are praying—
"Alas!—stroke! Why the rescue are you now
        delaying?"

DIONYSOS. Two strokes for you, Aeschylus.

EURIPIDES. "Learn from me, wide-ruling child,
1270       Atreides, noblest Achaian"—
"Alas!—stroke! Why the rescue are you now delaying?"

DIONYSOS. This is your third stroke, Aeschylus.

EURIPIDES. "Hold still! Bee-keepers of Artemis are
        near to begin the maying"—
1275 "Alas!—stroke! Why the rescue are you now delaying?"

"Mine is the power to shout the fated force of Greek
        foraging"—
"Alas!—stroke! Why the rescue are you now delaying?"

DIONYSOS. King Zeus, what a monster pile of strokes!   *[margin: trimeters]*
I want to go to the baths. My kidneys
1280 have puffed my groin with heatstroke.

EURIPIDES. Hear first another set of songs,
made of his lyre-played melodies.

DIONYSOS. Finish, but lay on no more strokes.

**1264–65, "O Phthian Achilles . . . man-slaying."** From Aeschylus'
lost *Myrmidons*. Achilles was from Phthia in northern Greece.
The second line will now be attached nonsensically to mock what
Euripides considers Aeschylus' incoherent style.
**1266, "To Hermes . . . praying."** From the lost *Ghost Raisers*.
**1270, "Learn . . . Achaian."** From the lost *Telephus* or *Iphigeneia*.
**1273–74, "Hold still . . . maying."** From the lost *Priestesses*.
*[margin: Ag. 104]* **1276, "Mine . . . foraging."** From the *Agamemnon* (104).

τὸ φλαττοθραττοφλαττόθρατ

mock
dactylic

EURIPIDES. "Thus the Achaian double-throned power,
  prime manhood of Greece,
Tophlattothrattophlattóthrat,
The Sphinx, dog-lord of cursed days, were sent,
Tophlattothrattophlattothrat,
With spear and with revenging hand by the ferocious
  bird,
Tophlattothrattophlattothrat,
Who let them with their eager air-roaming dogs light,
Tophlattothrattophlattothrat,
Upon those pressing against Ajax,
Tophlattothrattophlattothrat."

1285
tophlatto-
thratto-
phlattothrat

1290

1295

trimeters

DIONYSOS. What is this "phlattothrat"? Did you
  collect
your rope-twister songs at Marathon or where?
  AESCHYLUS. I brought them *from* Beauty *to* Beauty,
lest I be seen plucking the same
sacred meadow of the muses as Phrynichus.
*(pointing to* EURIPIDES*)*
*He* took honey from everywhere: whore-songs,
Meletus' drink-ups, Carian flute-songs,
laments, dances, as soon will be clear.

noble
source

1300

Someone bring my lyre. But why
are lyres needed? Where's the one who clicks
time with her castanets. Here, Muse of Euripides,
for whom it is proper to sing these songs.
*(Ugly* MUSE *appears briefly.)*

1305

**1285–95, "Thus . . . Tophlattothrattophlattothrat."** This wild far-
rago mixes lines from Aeschylus' *Agamemnon* (109–11) and a line
from his lost *Sphinx* with a nonsense refrain.
**1297, rope-twister songs at Marathon.** References to the folk songs
sung by rope-makers and to The Battle of Marathon (490 B.C.)
at which Aeschylus fought?
**1300, Phrynichus.** See note on line 910.
**1302, Meletus' drink-ups, Carian flute-songs.** Meletus was perhaps
the inferior tragedian who accused Socrates. **Carian.** From Caria
in Asia Minor (Turkey). The word must have suggested immo-
rality.

Ag: 109-11

104   *Aristophanes*

DIONYSOS. Ugh! This muse was no whore from
Lesbos!

AESCHYLUS.

"Kingfishers by the ever-fluent wave,     *mock Aeoli*

1310                     How you rave,
Wetting with wet wings,
Bedewing your bird-skin;
Spiders in the corners of the roof-tops,
You whose fingers wi-i-i-i-i-ind   *εἱειειειειΛίσσετε*

1315           The thread stretched on the loom,
Cares of the songful weaver-pin,
Whither yon flute-loving dolphin
Bounds to dark-blue bows,
Oracles and the race-track.

1320         Joyous the bloom of the vine,
Clustering tendril that stops all the pain.
Hug me, my child."

                 *τὸν πόδα τούς'*

*"feet"*   | Did you notice those feet?

DIONYSOS. (*misunderstanding, looking at* EURIPIDES' *(or girl's)*
    *real feet*)              I see.

AESCHYLUS. What *are* you doing? Notice those feet?

DIONYSOS.                                    I did.

AESCHYLUS.

1325             You wrote that mess of song?
And dared to find mine wrong?
You wrote with those twelve tics:
Cyrene's whorish tricks.

**1308, Lesbos.** In the fifth century, there were many prostitutes
from the island of Lesbos. There is no reference to "lesbians."
**1309–22, "Kingfishers . . . my child."** The following song shifts
rhythms and sense in order to parody Euripides' lyric measures.
The first four lines may parody Euripides' *Iphigeneia in Tauris*
(1089–1105), although an ancient commentator (scholiast) says
they are from Euripides' *Iphigeneia at Aulis*. The next four lines
contain even more uncertain references. The next two about the
dolphin are from Euripides' *Electra* (435–37). The references to
oracles and race-tracks is unknown. The next three refer to Euripides' lost *Hypsipyle*.
**1328, Cyrene.** A notorious and versatile prostitute.

*trimeter* Those are your choruses. I also wish
to go through your solo style:                                    1330

*Mock medley*

> "O gloom of night, that's darkling bright,     *tragic diction*
>                 What vision of                  *for trivial*
>          Disaster do you send,                   *incident*
>          Herald of hidden Hell,
>              A soul-less soul,
>     Black child of night, shuddering sight,      1335
>     Fierce black-clad corpse that flashes
>     Gore, gore and has big fingernails?

> "Servants, come quick and light the wick.
> In pitchers, raise the virgin river water, make it hot,
>     So I may scrub away my sacred dream.         1340
>                 O, spirit of the sea,
>     I've got it! O, my household friends,
>              Behold the signs:
>              Honey has gone
>     And made off with my rooster!
>     O mountain-nurtured nymphs,
>          O Mania, nab her!                        1345

>          "But I—oh my!—
>     By chance was at my task,
>          Wi-i-inding the flax *ειειει ειειλίσσουσα*
>          Full on the spindle,
>     Making the yarn with my two hands,
>     So I could bring it to the Agora             1350
>     Before the sun came up.

>     "It flew, it flew up to the blue
>     On lightest tips of wings,

**1331–64, "O gloom of night . . . the thief."** A satirical lyric follows, hinting at Euripidean style. Many of the references are
uncertain. For Euripides' Gothic style, cf. his *Orestes* (1369–1502),
which Aeschylus partly parodies here. Honey is the name of a
slave, as is Mania.

> Left me pain, pain,
> And wretched me, my eyes
1355        Shed, shed tears, tears.

> "O Cretans, offspring of Mount Ida, bring
> Your bows and help.
> On flying feet, surround my house
> And let the chase's child, beauteous Artemis
> Come too and race her tiny bitches through the
1360        rooms.

> "And you, Zeus-born, come too;
> Raise in your hands your twin most gleaming torches,
> O Hecate, and light my way to Honey's house,
> So I may enter in and catch the thief."

DIONYSOS.  Stop the songs!

AESCHYLUS.                    Enough too for me.

*put him to scales*

1365 | I want to put him in the scales.
     | It alone shall prove our poetry
     | and test the weight of our phrases.

DIONYSOS.  Come here then, if I too
must sell the poet's art like cheese.

*(A balance with scales is set up.)*

*EPISODE 2; ODE B*

1370   CHORUS.   The witty ones work hard.          *trochaic*
                This new thing's out of range
                And more than passing strange,
                Made only by these bards.

                Oh my! Not even after
1375            Some fellow took my sleeve
                And swore would I believe,
                But he would have my laughter.

*EPISODE 2 CONT.*

DIONYSOS.  Come, stand by the pans.          *trimeters*

AESCHYLUS *and* EURIPIDES.            There!

DIONYSOS.  Take them and each speak your phrase,
1380  but don't let it drop till I say, "Cuckoo!"

AESCHYLUS *and* EURIPIDES.  Got them!

DIONYSOS.              Recite your phrase in the scale.

*matching phrases, words*

EURIPIDES. "Would that the hull of Argo never ⌐ flew"—⌐ *Medea*

AESCHYLUS. "Spercheian River, cattle-grazing banks"—

DIONYSOS. Cuckoo! κοκκύ

AESCHYLUS *and* EURIPIDES. It's in.

DIONYSOS.                 Far lower
his goes down.

EURIPIDES.   For what reason?          1385

DIONYSOS. Why? He put in a river, like merchants,
wetting his words as they pad their wool.
You put in a winged word.

EURIPIDES. Let him speak another and stand the test.

DIONYSOS. Take your pan.

AESCHYLUS *and* EURIPIDES. Ready!

DIONYSOS.                Speak.        1390

EURIPIDES. "Persuasion's only temple is the word."

AESCHYLUS. "Death is the only god who loves no gift."

DIONYSOS. Let go!

AESCHYLUS *and* EURIPIDES. It's in.

DIONYSOS.               Again his sinks,
for he put death in, heaviest of evils.

EURIPIDES. And I persuasion, finest of expressions.  1395

DIONYSOS. Persuasion's light and has no sense.
But find another of more weight.
The strong and great will draw you down.

EURIPIDES. Where do I have one? Where?

DIONYSOS.                     I'll tell
                              you:

   "Achilles tossed two singles and a four."    1400

Speak now, for this is your last weighing.

**1382, "Would . . . flew."** From Euripides' *Medea* (1).
**1383, "Spercheian River . . . banks."** From Aeschylus' lost *Philoctetes*.
**1391, "Persuasion's . . . word."** From Euripides' lost *Antigone*.
**1392, "Death . . . gift."** From Aeschylus' lost *Niobe*.
**1400, "Achilles . . . four."** From Euripides' lost *Telephus*?

EURIPIDES. "He took in his right hand his iron club."
AESCHYLUS. "Chariot upon chariot and corpse on
corpse."
DIONYSOS. He tricked you again.
EURIPIDES.                    In what way?
1405    DIONYSOS. He put in two chariots and two corpses.
Not even a hundred Egyptians could lift that.
    AESCHYLUS. No more verse by verse, but in the scale
let him go sit and his children and wife
and her Cephisophon and take his books too.
1410    I'll speak only two lines—
    *(Enter* PLUTO.*)*
    DIONYSOS. Both are friends; I cannot judge.
I shall not fight with them.
For one I think wise; the other I love.
*Pluto*    PLUTO. Will you not do what you came for?
    DIONYSOS. And if I judge one better?
    PLUTO.                    Take back
1415    your choice, so you don't come in vain.
    DIONYSOS. Bless you! Come, hear me.
I came down for a poet.
    EURIPIDES.            For what?
    DIONYSOS. So the city be saved and lead her
    choruses.
1420    Whoever would advise the city well,
I would deem worthy to lead back.
First, what opinion do you each have
of Alcibiades, for the city is in labor.
    EURIPIDES. What is the city's opinion?
    DIONYSOS.                    Hers?
1425    She loves and hates and wants to have him.

**1402, "He ... club."** From Euripides' lost *Meleager*.
**1403, "Chariot ... corpse."** From Aeschylus' lost *Glaukus Pot-nieus*.
**1423, Alcibiades.** A glamorous, unscrupulous general and states-man of great ability. He was educated by Socrates and fought for, and against, Athens. The question of the day was whether to recall him from exile in order to aid the city.

But say what you think about him.

    EURIPIDES. I hate the man who's slow to aid
his native land, quick to harm,
resourceful for himself, not her.

    DIONYSOS. Good, by Poseidon. What is yours?

    AESCHYLUS. Rear *not* a lion in the city.
If one is reared, honor its ways.

    DIONYSOS. By Zeus our Savior, I am in a bind.
One speaks cleverly; the other clearly. *

        σοφῶς        σαφῶς

Each speak one thought for the city:
What plan do you have for her deliverance?

    EURIPIDES. If one made Cinesias the wings of
       Cleocritus,
breezes would lift them over the plain of the sea.

    DIONYSOS. It would seem funny. What does it mean?

    EURIPIDES. If they fight at sea, let them hold vinegar-
       jars
and bedaub the eyes of our enemies.

But I know and wish to say.

    DIONYSOS.             Speak.

    EURIPIDES. Now when we make the distrusted trusted
and the trusted distrusted—

    DIONYSOS.            What? I don't understand.
Speak less profoundly and more roundly.

    EURIPIDES. If those citizens we now trust
we would distrust, and we would use
those we don't, we would be saved.
If we are unlucky with these, how
doing the opposite can we *not* be saved?

    DIONYSOS. Good, O Palamedes, wisdom's self!

1430

1435

1440

1445

1450

**1437, Cinesias . . . Cleocritus.** For Cinesias, see note on line 153.
Cleocritus was supposed to resemble an ostrich (Aristophanes'
*Birds*, (l. 877).

**1451, Palamedes.** A resourceful Greek hero who fought against
the Trojans.

\* Poetry must teach and delight.

Did you discover this, or did Cephisophon?
EURIPIDES. I alone. Cephisophon did the vinegar-jars.
DIONYSOS. What about you? What do you say?
AESCHYLUS.                           Tell me
those the city employs, are they good?
1455    DIONYSOS.                           What!
She despises the good worst of all.
AESCHYLUS.                           And loves the bad?
DIONYSOS. Not her, but uses them through necessity.
AESCHYLUS. How can anyone save a city
that neither coat nor cloak fits?
1460    DIONYSOS. Find out, by Zeus, if you resurface.
AESCHYLUS. I would speak there, not here.
DIONYSOS. No, send your good news up!
AESCHYLUS. When they consider their enemy's land
their land and theirs the enemy's,
1465 when ships are wealth and wealth is poverty.
DIONYSOS. Good, but the juryman alone swigs all
    down.
PLUTO. Judge!
DIONYSOS.       This shall be my verdict:
I shall take back the one my soul desires.
EURIPIDES. Remember the gods you swore by
1470 to lead me back. Take your friends.
DIONYSOS. My *tongue* swore that . . . but I'll choose
    Aeschylus!
EURIPIDES. What have you done, O most-polluted
    man?
DIONYSOS. Me?
I judged Aeschylus winner. Why not?
EURIPIDES. You've done the basest deed, and look me
    in the face?
DIONYSOS. *(glancing at the audience)*
1475        "What shame if viewers think not so?"

(margin notes:)
city hates honest people
my tongue swore
Aesch. wins

(handwritten Greek note near line 1473:) διαισχιστον ἔργον

---

**1452, Cephisophon.** See note on line 944.
**1471, My *tongue* swore that.** Cf. line 102 and note.
**1475, "What shame . . . so."** A parody of a scandalous line from
Euripides' lost *Aeolus*: "What shame if doers think not so?"

*The Frogs*   111

EURIPIDES. Bastard, will you leave me dead?

DIONYSOS.  Who knows if living's also dying,

and breathing bread and sleep a fleece?

PLUTO.  Go in now, Dionysos.

DIONYSOS.                    Why?

PLUTO.  So I may host you before you sail.

DIONYSOS.                              Well said.   1480

By Zeus, I will not carp at that.

*(All exit but the* CHORUS.*)*                    STASIMON 2

*trochaic*   CHORUS.        Blessed is that man
                          Wit has made exact—
                          Learn it where we can.
                          Thinking well in fact,        1485
                          He returns to home,
                          Makes his people good.
                          He makes good his own
                          Kin and neighborhood.
                          Wisdom is his food.


                          Elegant it's not         1490   *criticizes*
                          Hearing Socrates,                *Socrates'*
                          Throwing down our art,           *students*
                          Scorning the verities
                          Of the tragic stage          1495
                          Scratching like a fool
                          On the holy page,
                          Making time a stool—
                          Mankind in a rage.

*(Enter* AESCHYLUS, DIONYSOS, PLUTO.*)*

    PLUTO. *(carrying a sword, nooses, and hemlock)*
*anap.*                   Come, farewell, Aeschylus.    1500 EXODOS
                          Go save that land of ours
                          With your fine thoughts and teach
                          The mindless who are many.

**1477, Who knows . . . dying.** Said by characters in Euripides' lost
*Polyidus, Erectheus,* and *Phrixus.*
**1492, Socrates.** For Aristophanes' comic view of Socrates as a
hairsplitting philosopher, cf. his *Clouds.*

|       |            | Give these to Cleophon, |
|-------|------------|--------------------------|
| 1505  |            | To tax commissioners, to |
|       |            | Nichomachus and Myrmex, |
|       |            | Archenomus, and say, |
|       |            | Come quickly here to me |
|       |            | Without delay. If they |
| 1510  |            | Won't come quick, by Apollo, |
|       |            | I'll brand them, tie their feet. |
|       |            | With Whitecrest's son, the traitor, |
|       |            | I'll send them quickly down. |

*Aesch. gives chair to Sophocles*

1515    AESCHYLUS.    I shall. Please hand my chair
                     To Sophocles to hold
                     And to protect if I
                     Return again. For I
                     Judge him the second wit.
1520                 Take heed that roguish man,
                     That lying sacrilege,
                     Never sits in my seat,
                     Not even if by chance.

        PLUTO.       Show him your holy torches!
1525                 Escort him on the way:
                     Sing loudly this man's songs
                     And celebrate his dances.

        CHORUS.
                     First bid good journey to our parting poet,    *dact.*
                     Who rises to the light, Ye Gods of Hell,
1530                 And good thoughts to the city of great goodness.

*No more war*

                     Let's stop the great distress entirely
                     And painful clash of arms. Let Cleophon
                     Go fight, and others willing, in *their* homelands.
        (*All exit.*)

---

**1506–07, Nichomachus and Myrmex,/Archenomus.** These three contemporary references are uncertain.

**1512, Whitecrest's son.** Adeimantus, a contemporary general. His father's comic name indicates pomposity.

**1532, Go fight . . . homelands.** A final gibe at the war party and its demagogue, Cleophon. Cf. note on line 679.

# selected bibliography

## the bacchae

L'*Année Philologique* provides an annual bibliography of works on Euripides.

Arnott, P. D. *Public and Performance in the Greek Theatre* (1989).

Bieber, M. *The History of the Greek and Roman Theater*. 2nd ed. (1961).

Collard, C. *Euripides* (1981).

Conacher, D. J. *Euripidean Drama: Myth, Theme, and Structure* (1967).

Dodds, E. R. *Euripides: Bacchae*. Edited with a Commentary. 2nd ed. (1960).

Dodds, E. R. *The Greeks and the Irrational* (1951).

Grube, G. M. A. *The Drama of Euripides* (1941).

Kerenyi, C. *Dionysos: Archetypal Image of Indestructible Life* (1976).

Murray, Gilbert, *Euripides and his Age* (1913).

Otto, W. F. *Dionysus: Myth and Cult* (1933; tr. 1965).

Oranje, Hans. *Euripides' Bacchae; The Play and its Audience* (1984).

Pickard-Cambridge, A. W. *Dramatic Festivals of Athens*. 2nd ed. J. Gould and D. M. Lewis (1968).

Segal, Charles. *Dionysian Poetics and Euripides' Bacchae* (1982).

Webster, T. B. L. *The Tragedies of Euripides* (1967).

Winnington-Ingram, R. P. *Euripides and Dionysus: An Interpretation of the Bacchae* (1948).

# the frogs

*L'Année Philologique* provides an annual bibliography of works on Aristophanes.

Bieber, M. *The History of the Greek and Roman Theatre.* 2nd ed. (1961).

Cornford, F. M. *The Origin of Attic Comedy.* Ed. Theodore H. Gaster (1961).

Coulon, V. *Aristophane.* Ed. with French Commentary. French translation by H. Van Daele (1952–54).

Dearden, C. W. *The Stage of Aristophanes* (1976).

Del Corno, Dario. *Aristophane: Le Rane.* Ed. with Italian Commentary and Translation (1985).

Dover, K. J. *Aristophanic Comedy* (1972).

Ehrenberg, Victor. *The People of Aristophanes.* 2nd ed. (1951).

Harriott, Rosemary. *Aristophanes: Poet and Dramatist* (1986).

Littlefield, D. J., ed. *Twentieth Century Interpretations of the Frogs. A Collection of Critical Essays* (1968).

MacLeish, K. *The Theatre of Aristophanes* (1980).

Murray, Gilbert. *Aristophanes* (1933).

Murray, Gilbert. *The Frogs.* Translation (1908).

Pickard-Cambridge, A. W. *The Dramatic Festivals of Athens.* 2nd ed. J. Gould and D. M. Lewis. (1968).

Rogers, B. B. *The Comedies of Aristophanes.* Ed. with Commentary and English Translation (1902–16).

Solomos, Alexis. *The Living Aristophanes* (1974).

Stanford, W. B. *Aristophanes: The Frogs.* Edited with a Commentary. 2nd ed. (1963).

Whitman, C. H. *Aristophanes and the Comic Hero* (1964).